THE ROYAL BALLET

A PICTURE HISTORY

THE ROYAL BALLET

A PICTURE HISTORY

Kathrine Sorley Walker and Sarah C. Woodcock

Threshold/Corgi

Never mind the money—give me those Sadler's Wells ballet tickets.

Cartoon which appeared in the Ottawa Star during the Company's first tour of North America in 1949.

Front cover: *The Dream*, Antoinette Sibley and Anthony Dowell
(Photograph: Houston Rogers)
Back cover: *Romeo and Juliet*, The Ballroom Scene (Photograph: Zoë Dominic)

THE ROYAL BALLET – A Picture History

A CORGI BOOK (in association with Threshold Books Ltd.) 0 552 98200 8
Produced by Threshold Books Limited

While research was in progress for the official history of the Company, *The Royal Ballet – The First 50 Years* by Alexander Bland, it was decided to create a companion volume from the wealth of excellent photographs and other illustrations that had been assembled.
This book, *The Royal Ballet – A Picture History,* is the result. The Publisher acknowledges with thanks the help given in the compilation of the book by the Royal Opera House.

Corgi edition published 1981
Copyright © Threshold Books Limited 1981

Text by Kathrine Sorley Walker
Picture research by Sarah C. Woodcock
Edited by Barbara Cooper
Designed by Karen Bowen

Corgi Books are published by Transworld Publishers Ltd.,
Century House, 61–63 Uxbridge Road, Ealing, London W5 5SA.
Set in Monophoto Optima. Made and printed in Great Britain by Balding & Mansell, Wisbech, Cambridgeshire.

INTRODUCTION

A Golden Jubilee means a celebration of continuity and development, an estimate of present status and past accomplishment. It is an occasion for looking back and forward, analysing, exploring and perhaps above all reminiscing. With The Royal Ballet there will be as many ways of doing this as there are individuals concerned.

Everyone who has been drawn into the Company's orbit in its fifty years of life, whether they have been professionally connected with it or are part of its worldwide public, will see the anniversary differently. They are not only geographically widely separate, their time span is long. Although they have an overall kinship of interest, their areas of enthusiasm and loyalty vary enormously.

The London audience of today at the Royal Opera House or Sadler's Wells Theatre, eagerly discussing the artistic development of current principals, seeking out ballerina material in new young dancers, is half a century away from those who remember the pioneers of the early thirties. A few people, of course, have travelled the whole road, but far more belong to some particular era. From this they have favourite ballets, much loved dancers, remembered or forgotten by those who write the histories. What they all share is the fact that at different times and in different places they have experienced some powerful magnetism, reaching out from the stage to the auditorium, that has won their affection and given them a feeling of identity with this remarkable organisation that grew from a modest nativity at the Old Vic on 5 May, 1931.

My own first memories of the Company are schoolgirl impressions of the 1939 *Sleeping Princess* at Sadler's Wells – a foggy February evening made bright by the marvellous harmonies of Petipa and Tchaikovsky as interpreted by Fonteyn and Helpmann – and a double bill of *Giselle* and *Checkmate* that opened my eyes to ballet's great range of possible pleasures. Then, during the wartime seasons at the New Theatre in London, I became deeply and irrevocably recruited to the Company's regular audience, going night after night in defiance of incendiary bombs, flying bombs and V2 rockets. These performances became a way of life for me, as they did for many others, and their quality repaid the sacrifices of time, money and energy that they involved.

Such intensive commitment could hardly continue for ever and as time went on it was replaced by a more moderate mood. A keen and lasting interest remained, however – a feeling of family that still exists, making me anxious and dismayed during problem patches of Company history and delighted when I am rewarded by performances and ballets of superb calibre.

The basic success story of The Royal Ballet is familiar and falls easily into stages. Initially the budding Vic-Wells Ballet depended on established principal dancers, particularly on Alicia Markova and Anton Dolin. After their departure in 1935, until 1945, when the Sadler's Wells Ballet transferred to the Royal Opera House, there was a vital period of artistic activity, stimulated rather than stunted by the dangers and hardships of World War II. The Company's own principals emerged, with Margot Fonteyn and Robert Helpmann as accepted leaders, and exciting choreographic work from Frederick Ashton, de Valois and Helpmann gave the Company a firm character in the public mind. Without this there would never have been the important invitation to Covent Garden when it reopened in February 1946.

From then the road divides. There is the Covent Garden Company and there is the Sadler's Wells venture, which must for convenience be termed 'the Touring Company' to cover its many name changes, which gave its first performances at Sadler's Wells Theatre in April 1946 and is now back there as Sadler's Wells Royal Ballet.

At Covent Garden during the later forties and fifties there were problems of adaptation to the larger house both for repertoire and dancers. This was the period of a return to full-length new ballets, with Ashton's *Cinderella, Sylvia* and *Ondine*; the period of the Massine revivals, of guest artists such as Alexandra Danilova and Frederic Franklin, of the conquest of New York and of the Royal Charter. At Sadler's Wells there were even more salutory events from the standpoint of future health in the steady development of choreographers – John Cranko and Kenneth MacMillan – and dancers – Svetlana Beriosova, Nadia Nerina, David Blair.

The next decade began with enormous promise at Covent Garden when Ashton's enchanting *La Fille Mal Gardée* was produced in January 1960. It marked a new phase of inventive power in this incomparable choreographer, who is a particular glory of our native ballet, a prolific and superbly versatile creator of either pure dance or dance narrative.

The sixties were also MacMillan years in which the three main streams of his personal style were clearly exemplified. *The Rite of Spring* and *Song of the Earth* proved his ability to compose richly expressive choreography to great music; *The Invitation* represented the preoccupation with psychological and sexual abnormalities that links him with modern permissive society; while *Romeo and Juliet* became the forerunner of the full-length dance drama focused on successive pas de deux that would become especially identified with him.

For many, however, the sixties were predominantly dancing years. Rudolf Nureyev's spectacular advent in 1962 and his glamorous international partnership with Fonteyn was only one aspect of this. There were other great guest artists in Yvette Chauviré and Erik Bruhn. More important for the Company's welfare, new principals of exceptional gifts were emerging from the Royal Ballet School.

There had been a school from the earliest days. Now for some years it had been a two-level organisation with a Junior School at White Lodge, Richmond and an Upper School at Baron's Court. Its methods produced an outstanding vintage at this time in Lynn Seymour, Antoinette Sibley, Merle Park, Doreen Wells, Anthony Dowell and David Wall, and their appearance made the sixties a halcyon time for all lovers of great classical dancing.

Early in the sixties came de Valois' retirement, a well-calculated step, although for many it seemed premature. Ashton's appointment as successor, with the backing of a capable triumvirate of Assistant Directors (Michael Somes, John Hart and John Field), meant a smooth continuation of policy until Ashton's own retirement in 1970.

This, however, will undoubtedly be seen in the long term as a sharp dividing line. The more revolutionary new ideas introduced under Kenneth MacMillan's directorship, such as the replacement of John Field's Touring Company, whose loss was widely regretted, with the experimental New Group, were shortlived. All the same, a glance at the recent history of both Companies shows how the image of The Royal Ballet has been changing – an inevitable state of affairs, naturally, in a cultural and social world pressured by inflation and conditioned by radically altered values and opinions.

The seventies have been years of acquisition as much as creation. The Royal Ballet has imported works by George Balanchine, Jerome Robbins, John Cranko, Glen Tetley, Hans van Manen, Herbert Ross, Antony Tudor and Ronald Hynd that have been originally staged by other companies. Even some of MacMillan's ballets originated abroad. One or two choreographers from outside have agreed to work creatively with the Company and MacMillan, fortunately, has been capable of continuous productivity. It is of importance that dancers should learn to adapt to many choreographic styles, but working with a choreographer on a new creation is an invaluable exercise at every stage of a dancer's career. There has also been a conscious effort to go beyond the classical image of the Company to reflect current trends of choreographic melding of classical and modern techniques, in the commissioning of works such as Tetley's *Field Figures* and *Dances of Albion*.

Finding new choreographers is universally agreed to be one of the biggest problems in ballet and there has always been concern as to who might be the heirs of the eighties. Looking at the record, The Royal Ballet can be seen to have worked at the task. Thanks to Leslie Edwards' admirably sustained Royal Ballet Choreographic Group, a good many young dancers have had the chance to try composition and some of them have been encouraged professionally. Since 1970 the Touring Company – the natural ground, as was once the Sadler's Wells Theatre Ballet, for this essential activity – has staged ballets by Geoffrey Cauley, David Drew, David Morse, Ashley Killar, Lynn Seymour, David Bintley and Michael Corder. The best contestants at the moment would seem to be Bintley and Corder; Bintley has produced seven ballets in two years, with varying degrees of success.

To sustain the high reputation of a ballet company not only choreographers are needed, and the seventies saw some decline in the strength and depth of the available dancing talent. The newer principals are all capable of giving, in certain roles and on certain occasions, performances of great sensitivity and technical skill. What most of them have not yet found is the emotional and dramatic power to lift these performances onto the level that their great predecessors achieved. Curiously, though in the sixties the impact of Nureyev's dancing provided an obvious stimulus, the same effect was not achieved through the guest appearances of Natalia Makarova and Mikhail Baryshnikov in the seventies.

New names are finding their way into programmes, press notices and conversations, and hopes are being built on young soloists of both sexes. However well they grasp their opportunities, they are all some way from displaying the stamina and sure command of the stage that has to be the basis for greatness, and there is a very British reserve in the way they present their meticulously schooled dancing. All the same, they are the future of The Royal Ballet, the personalities who must carry this magnificent Company over the fiftieth anniversary towards the century, following, after their own fashion and within the demands of contemporary society, the superb achievements of the founders and pathfinders.

The Royal Ballet of today, in its dual character, has little similarity to the Company that went to Covent Garden in 1945. The repertoire has few links with the distant past except for a few enduring works by de Valois and Ashton. This is nothing to mourn. Times change and, more importantly, the abilities and outlook of dancers change, and the great pre-war or wartime ballets which some of us cherish in memory cannot be convincingly staged by present-day artists. The productions of the classics are constantly under revision – often, one feels, unnecessarily or for the worse; but revision is a sign of life, and there is now the assurance that what is replaced is preserved by the choreologist. Some of the new readings, such as Peter Wright's *Giselle* for the Touring Company, are a delight.

The approach to the collaborative arts of music and design has changed. Commissioned scores are now very rare, and studio painters of renown are seldom brought into the theatre. However, the standard of design remains satisfactorily high in a balletic world that tends all too often to feature uninteresting or tasteless costumes and sets. In common with other companies, technique has become more gymnastic and acrobatic, and demi-caractère is largely a lost art.

All ballet companies of artistic maturity have their own character. The Royal Ballet's lies partly in its technical style, which is fluent rather than brilliant, lyrical rather than flamboyant, neat rather than ample in its approach to steps and gesture. There is a general moderation and reserve in presentation – a very English attribute – but the greatest Royal Ballet artists transcend such limitations and achieve heights of virtuosity both in technique and in interpretation. Royal Ballet dancers are extremely adaptable. They are, somewhat naturally, at their best in ballets by their own choreographers, especially Ashton and MacMillan, but they are capable of giving creditable accounts of works by choreographers as disparate as Jerome Robbins and Glen Tetley. They have a strong tradition of dramatic dancing, happily maintained in current performance, and an equally high reputation for preserving and presenting the inherited 19th-century repertoire. These magnificent ballets are the touchstone of the classical dancer's art, and from the beginning the Company has been their principal custodian in the West.

One special characteristic bridges the years, the best christening gift that any cradle can receive – the gift of comedy in all its aspects, wit, humour, clowning and farce. No one who loves this Company could consider its Golden Jubilee without remembering laughter as much as cathartic tragedy or virtuoso excitement. Comedy took the stage as early as *Regatta* and is still flourishing at both Covent Garden and Sadler's Wells.

Who are the dancers who have amused us most, who have lifted the gloom of everyday life and personal distress? I have my own answer to this, and each reader will agree and disagree and get out his pen to make a rival list. For me, some highlights (which inevitably leave many memorable chuckles unchronicled) are : Helpmann as O'Reilly, Holden in *Selina*, Emblen as the Widow Simone ; Seymour in the flirtation solo of *Dances at a Gathering* ;

Parkinson and Fletcher in *The Concert,* Mason and Wall in the drunk duet in *Manon* ; Jefferies and Barbieri in *Card Game* ; above all, perhaps, the Knights Grand Cross of Comedy – Ashton and Helpmann as Cinderella's Stepsisters.

Like this list, a picture history of the fifty years is bound to be controversial. Space is short. So many ballets, so many performances, have to be left out. No one will find all that he wants in these pages, but if some memories are stirred, some pleasures recaptured and some links of development and chronology made clear, it will strengthen the essential links between The Royal Ballet and its audience.

A montage, made in 1971, of principal dancers of The Royal Ballet.

EARLY YEARS

(Above) Advertisement from The Dancing Times, 1917.
(Right) Ninette de Valois as principal dancer in 'Aïda' at the Royal Opera House in 1919. (Below) Newspaper advertisement for a variety bill at the London Coliseum, 1922.
(Opposite) 1923 revival of 'Narcisse' by Serge Diaghilev's Ballets Russes. Ninette de Valois (standing, at left) with Maikerska (Nymph) and Taddeus Slavinsky (Narcisse).

Pride of place in this pictorial record of the Royal Ballet must go to Dame Ninette de Valois, DBE. To its creation she brought widely varied theatrical experience.

Wicklow-born to a non-theatrical family (her original name was Edris Stannus), she had such a natural gift for dancing that when she was fourteen she was touring England with The Wonder Children from the Lila Field Academy.

From 1914–19 she was principal dancer in the Lyceum Theatre Christmas pantomime and in summer 1919 première danseuse of the first post-World War I International Season of Grand Opera at the Royal Opera House, Covent Garden. She appeared in musical comedies and revues, and in variety on the same bill as celebrated music hall artists such as Little Tich and George Robey.

Her studies with the great ballet master Enrico Cecchetti led her to the Diaghilev Ballets Russes in September 1923. There she worked with Nijinska, Massine and Balanchine, as well as learning the classic and Fokine repertoire. She danced in the corps de ballet and in small solo roles such as Papillon in *Carnaval* and the Finger variation in *Aurora's Wedding*.

To be part of such a great organisation was vital to her artistic development. She observed the life and construction of the Diaghilev Ballet with a receptive and critical eye, and she formulated firm ideas about the kind of ballet company that she wanted to build up in England.

Two other exceptional people joined de Valois as architects of The Royal Ballet : Frederick Ashton and Constant Lambert. Ashton, influenced by seeing Pavlova in Peru, quitted without reluctance an office job in London to study with Massine and later with Marie Rambert.

Rambert's creative attitude towards young artists – her students then included two other future choreographers, Antony Tudor and Andrée Howard – guided Ashton's career. In 1926 he composed his first ballet, *A Tragedy of Fashion*, for the Rambert dancers to perform in Sir Nigel Playfair's revue *Riverside Nights* at the Lyric Theatre, Hammersmith.

Two years later Ashton joined the Ida Rubinstein Ballet in Paris, where Nijinska, as Ballet Mistress, had engaged a remarkable group of young male dancers, among them David Lichine and Yurek Shabelevsky. In Nijinska Ashton found an excitingly stylish romanticism that would influence much of his later work.

Both before and after Rubinstein, Ashton created ballet scenes in West End productions like *Jew Süss* (1929) or Cochran's *The Cat and the Fiddle* (1932), learning valuable lessons of theatrecraft from this contact with the commercial stage.

Lambert, son of a well-known Australian artist, Maurice Lambert, won a scholarship to the Royal College of Music in 1922, and in 1926 the Diaghilev Ballet staged Nijinska's *Romeo and Juliet* to a score by him which he had originally called *Adam and Eve*. This was followed by two other compositions later mounted as ballets, *Pomona* (1926) and *The Rio Grande* (1927).

Lambert's great gift for friendship made him part of a circle of brilliant personalities – composers, artists and writers – and ensured that he, and through him the Vic-Wells Ballet, was completely integrated with the exciting English cultural world of the time.

(Opposite, above) 'A Tragedy of Fashion'. Frederick Ashton, centre, as Monsieur Duchic, Marie Rambert as Orchidée. Left to right, Elizabeth Vincent as Désir du Cygne, Esme Biddle as Viscountess Viscosa, W. Earle Grey as Viscount Viscosa, Frances James as Rose d'Ispahan. (Opposite, below) 'The Passionate Pilgrim', Ashton's contribution to 'The Cat and the Fiddle'. Left to right : Eric Marshall as Harlequin, Alice Delysia as Pierrot, Muriel Barron as Pierrette. (Left) Constant Lambert. (Below, left) Ashton, fourth from right, with the Ida Rubinstein company in 1929 ; on his right is Bronislav Nijinska ; the group also includes David Lachine, William Chappell and Rupert Doone. (Right) Review from The Times, 23 June 1926.

THE RUSSIAN BALLET.

"ROMEO AND JULIET."

Mr. Constant Lambert's ballet *Romeo and Juliet* was produced at His Majesty's Theatre on Monday night for the first time in England. It is the first occasion on which M. Diaghilev has used music by an Englishman for one of his productions. One wishes that Mr. Lambert had seized the opportunity of writing music which could be called definitely English. He seems rather to have chosen to speak to us in French, and, like many foreigners, he speaks it even better than the Frenchman. At any rate, it contrasted very favourably with a tedious little piece by M. Auric, which was played as an *entr'acte*.

EARLY YEARS

After leaving the Diaghilev Ballet in 1925, de Valois established her own studio, the Academy of Choreographic Art, in Roland Gardens, South Kensington, in March 1926. Ursula Moreton, who had also danced with the Ballets Russes, was Assistant Principal. Soon afterwards de Valois had her historic meeting with Lilian Baylis of the Old Vic, who engaged her to teach and arrange dances at that theatre.

Within the next year or two de Valois began choreographing for two progressive theatres, the Festival Theatre, Cambridge, and the Abbey Theatre, Dublin.

The Festival Theatre director was her cousin Terence Gray, and the plays included *The Oresteia*. At the Abbey Theatre she worked on productions of W.B. Yeats' *Plays for Dancers*. Both tasks encouraged the strong, serious, dramatic mood that characterise her greatest ballets, *Job*, *Checkmate* and *The Rake's Progress*.

She was an avant-garde choreographer. *Rout* (1928) was linked to an Ernst Toller poem and dealt with youth's revolt against conventional attitudes. Its choreography was modern in style and sculptural in

groupings. The same year the first ballet was given at the Old Vic – de Valois' *Les Petits Riens*, a pastoral piece to Mozart used as a curtain raiser to *Hansel and Gretel*.

The need to acquire a second theatre, to do justice to both drama and opera and to make possible the founding of a ballet company, was keenly felt by Lilian Baylis. Sir Reginald Rowe, a Governor of the Old Vic, suggested that they might buy and restore the ruined but famous Sadler's Wells Theatre in Islington, and Baylis saw the potential of the derelict building.

The theatre's origins lay in the discovery of a medicinal spring in 1683, which an enterprising Mr Sadler promoted by creating a pleasure garden and music house. The first theatre was built by Rosoman in 1765 and was home to the great clown Grimaldi before it became an aquatic theatre under Dibdin. Its most notable period had been in the 1850s and 60s under Phelps. After that its decline was steady – from 1915 it was abandoned – but in March 1925 a financial appeal was launched and by 1930 the re-building was in hand.

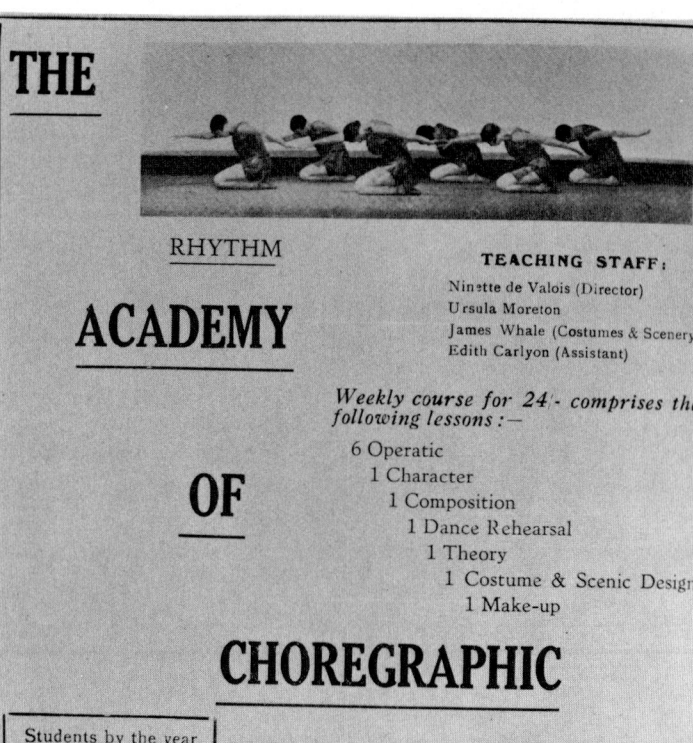

THE

RHYTHM

ACADEMY

OF

CHOREGRAPHIC

ART

TEACHING STAFF:
Ninette de Valois (Director)
Ursula Moreton
James Whale (Costumes & Scenery)
Edith Carlyon (Assistant)

Weekly course for 24/- comprises the following lessons :—

6 Operatic
1 Character
1 Composition
1 Dance Rehearsal
1 Theory
1 Costume & Scenic Design
1 Make-up

Students by the year taken *inclusively* for £40

The choregraphic work for the following list of Productions from November 1926 to November 1927 has been under the direction of this Academy.

OLD VIC.
"Midsummer Night's Dream"
"The Tempest"
"A Winter's Tale"
"Christmas Play"
"Taming of the Shrew"
"Much Ado about Nothing"

FESTIVAL THEATRE, CAMBRIDGE.
"The Oresteia"
"Rout" ballet by A. Bliss
"The Immortal Hour"
"Love for Love"
"Six Dance Cameos"
"Œdipus Tyrannus"
"Three Dance Studies"

THE FORUM THEATRE GUILD
The Beggars' Dance in "The Dybbuk"

LONDON COLISEUM
Dances for Anton Dolin's Company

THE MUSIC CLUB
Dance Programme

NOTE
The Academy will give its first series of PUBLIC PERFORMANCES early in the New Year.

(Opposite, top) Advertisement from
The Dancing Times. (Opposite, left)
Lilian Baylis, at centre, in the
wardrobe at the Old Vic. (Opposite,
right) Scene from 'Rout' produced at
the Festival Theatre, Cambridge, in
1928.
(Above) 'Les Petits Riens'. Ursula
Moreton is at centre. (Right) Sadler's
Wells Theatre in 1926.

EARLY YEARS

The restored Sadler's Wells Theatre was opened on Twelfth Night, 6 January, 1931 with a performance of Shakespeare's *Twelfth Night*. At first, opera and drama alternated between the Old Vic and Sadler's Wells. The six dancers, plus de Valois and male guest artists, were mainly employed in operas, but by May, Baylis agreed to risk one complete evening of ballet.

This was staged at the Old Vic. One of the ballets, *Danse Sacrée et Danse Profane,* had been created by de Valois for the Camargo Society in 1930. This pioneer venture, made possible by Philip Richardson, Editor of 'The Dancing Times', Arnold Haskell and John Maynard (later Lord) Keynes, was launched in October 1930 and gave intermittent performances until 1933. It proved an admirable showcase for British balletic talent. Many of its premièred works were later added to the Vic-Wells Ballet repertoire, and the cash in hand at its closure was devoted to the production in 1936 of Ashton's *Apparitions.*

5 May, 1931 was also Anton Dolin's first guest appearance with the Vic-Wells Ballet, in *Suite of Dances* (Bach/de Valois) and his own solo *Spanish Dance.*

The new régime at Sadler's Wells not only included the nucleus of a regular ballet company ; the school run by de Valois was transferred from Kensington to Islington. The profits from the school were devoted to the Company's development, as were the proceeds of the regular ballet classes for office workers.

(Above) Sadler's Wells Theatre in 1931. (Right) Photograph published in The Times on 3 January 1931 of a scene from the opera 'Carmen'. (Opposite, top left) Programme for the first full evening of ballet at the Old Vic on 5 May 1931. (Opposite, top right) Advertisement for the Vic-Wells School which appeared in Old Vic/Sadler's Wells programmes in 1931. (Opposite, below) Scene from 'Danse Sacrée et Danse Profane'.

" CARMEN " BALLET.—Miss Ninette de Valois (centre), principal dancer, with the ballet to appear in the performance of *Carmen* by the Old Vic opera company on Monday next.

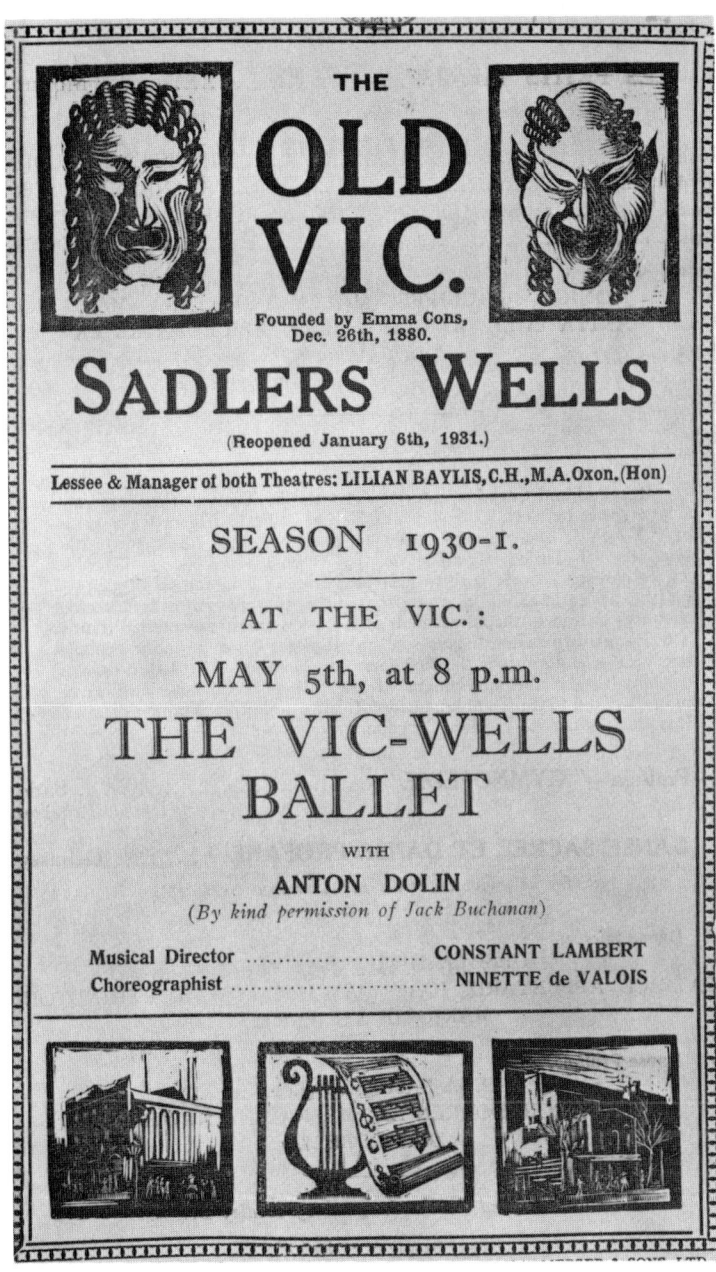

TEACHING BALLET-GOERS TO DANCE

VIC-WELLS School of Ballet.

The acquisition of the Sadler's Wells Theatre enables the organisation to include a permanent Opera Ballet of trained dancers with Ninette de Valois as prima ballerina and choreographist. There is a school of ballet attached to the theatre for the express purpose of making English ballet a feature of the two theatres. The proceeds of the school will be devoted to the upkeep and enlargement of the Opera Ballet Company. There will also be two classes per week held at The Old Vic in the evenings for office workers.

1931–1933

Star names were important in consolidating the new Company's reputation. Alicia Markova, Lydia Lopokova, Anton Dolin and Stanislas Idzikovsky were early guests, and Markova joined the Company as prima ballerina in 1933.

Job, the de Valois ballet in which Dolin made a striking success as Satan, had been staged for the Camargo Society two months before it was given at the Old Vic (September 1931). It used the magnificent score by Ralph Vaughan Williams and had designs by Gwen Raverat, based on Blake. Stanley Judson, who had danced with Pavlova, was Elihu.

Markova, a Londoner trained by Astafieva and engaged by Diaghilev in 1924 when she was only fourteen, had danced with the Camargo Society and with Marie Rambert's Ballet Club. She mounted Les Sylphides for the Vic-Wells Ballet in 1932, based on memories of the Diaghilev production.

Ashton staged his first ballet for the Company on 22 September, 1931. This was an amusing trifle, Regatta, to a score by Gavin Gordon with designs by William Chappell. Gordon had been Lambert's contemporary at the Royal College of Music; Chappell, like Ashton, was with Rambert and Ida Rubinstein.

Both Regatta and Job were shown in Copenhagen when the Vic-Wells contributed to a British ballet season organised by de Valois for the Association of Operatic Dancing of Great Britain (now the Royal Academy of Dancing) to coincide with a British Trades and Arts Exhibition in June/July 1932 – the first overseas tour undertaken by an all-British ballet company.

De Valois was the Vic-Wells' chief choreographer, and in October 1932 she staged a typically lively work, Douanes, to a score by Geoffrey Toye. Lambert had been engaged as conductor and Music Director in 1931, and new music was very much part of the creative policy. In Douanes, character sketches of gendarmes and customs men, supporting the leading roles of a Tightrope Dancer and Cook's Man, declared a debt to Massine. It was influenced, but in no way derivative, bearing de Valois' clear personal signature.

On 21 March, 1933 the Company staged the two-act version of Coppélia, a ballet mainly identified in London with Adeline Genée and the Empire Theatre. This time it was based on the Maryinsky Theatre version credited to Petipa and Ivanov, and it was revived by the Russian régisseur Nicholas Sergeyev. Lopokova alternated with de Valois as Swanilda. Judson was Franz and Hedley Briggs Dr Coppélius – both roles carefully watched by a new boy in the corps de ballet, Robert Helpmann who had been a student dancer with Pavlova in Australia. Six months later, he took a first step to stardom in Job.

(Opposite, top left) Anton Dolin as Satan in 'Job'; (top right) Ailne Phillips, Ursula Moreton, Stanley Judson and Beatrice Appleyard in 'Les Sylphides'; (below) Sheila McCarthy, Freda Bamford and Joy Newton in 'Regatta'.
(Left, above) 'Coppélia', with Stanley Judson as Franz, Lydia Lopokova as Swanilda and Hedley Briggs as Dr Coppélius; (below) 'Douanes', with Anton Dolin as Cook's Man, Ninette de Valois as the Tightrope Dancer, Claude Newman, Travis Kemp and Guy Massey as Gendarmes.

5 December, 1933 saw the première of Ashton's *Les Rendezvous* – he was now listed in the programme with de Valois as a 'choreographist'. A pleasure from the start, *Les Rendezvous* remains in the repertoire of Sadler's Wells Royal Ballet. Chappell, by then a member of the Company, designed the men's costumes with striped or wavy-lined tights that hardly flattered brilliant little Idzikovsky's muscly legs. Markova, however, had a charming grey-blue dress with a headdress of scarlet roses. The score, from Auber's 'L'Enfant Prodigue', was arranged by Lambert, a proof of his singular gift for this kind of compilation.

Two more long classic revivals were made possible by Markova and Dolin with Sergeyev. *Giselle* and *Casse-Noisette* were staged in January 1934. Markova was only twenty-three, and initiated in *Giselle* a performance that would become legendary on both sides of the Atlantic. Hermione Darnborough was Myrtha and Helpmann Hilarion.

Casse-Noisette was the largest production to date, with many extra performers, some from the Lord Mayor's Boy Players. Markova was an enchanting Sugar Plum Fairy, partnered by Judson. An unorthodox casting by Sergeyev gave actress Elsa Lanchester the Danse Arabe. She was then acting Ariel to the Prospero of her husband, Charles Laughton, in an Old Vic production of *The Tempest*.

(Above, left) Alicia Markova and Stanislas Idzikowsky in 'Les Rendezvous', (Above, right) Elsa Lanchester performing the Danse Arabe in 'Casse-Noisette'. (Left) Alicia Markova as Giselle, Anton Dolin as Albrecht, in the redesigned production of 1935. (Opposite page) Scene from 'Casse-Noisette', with Markova as the Sugar Plum Fairy, Stanley Judson as the Nutcracker Prince; on the floor, Elizabeth Miller and Ailne Phillips; with Gwyneth Mathews and Joy Newton, Hermione Darnborough and Beatrice Appleyard.

Dolin's connection with the Vic-Wells Ballet had been punctuated by other engagements, and in 1934 de Valois inaugurated a partnership between Markova and the rapidly improving Helpmann. In April she choreographed *The Haunted Ballroom,* a Gothic tale of doom that exploited Helpmann's fine sense of drama and physical grace. Markova was perfectly cast in the light and shadowy role of the ghost-heroine. Before long the small part of the son was taken by the fifteen-year-old Margot Fontes, soon to be known as Fonteyn.

In October Markova and Helpmann reinforced their partnership in *Giselle,* and in November in the important revival of the full length *Le Lac des Cygnes.* It was the first time that the ballet had been seen in England in its entirety, and it was a triumph. Markova's Odette-Odile was greatly praised and Helpmann had an acting, dancing and partnering success as Siegfried.

(Left) 'The Haunted Ballroom'; at left, William Chappell as the Stranger Player; at right, Alicia Markova as Alicia, Robert Helpmann as Master of Tregennis. (Right) Markova as Columbine, Helpmann as Harlequin, Claude Newman as Pantalon in 'Carnaval', 1934. (Below) Markova as Odette, Helpmann as Prince Siegfried and William Chappell as Benno in Act II of 'Le Lac des Cygnes'.

1935

Markova was restless, as most leading dancers limited to very small salaries must become, and de Valois gave thought to the succession. Three young dancers were promising: Elizabeth Miller, Pamela May and Margot Fonteyn. The last, in racing parlance, was the favourite, and at fifteen she proved her potential by dancing the Creole Girl in Ashton's *Rio Grande,* a Camargo Society acquisition staged in March 1935. She was also dancing the lead in the opera 'Aïda'.

Meanwhile the Company received an unusual offer. Mrs Laura Henderson, owner of the Windmill Theatre, and Vivian Van Damm, its general manager, proposed to back a tour for the Vic-Wells Ballet with Markova and Helpmann as stars. Helpmann, however, had signed up to appear in the revue *Stop Press,* so Dolin replaced him in the special

short seasons at the Wells, at the (now vanished) Shaftesbury Theatre, and in the provincial tour that followed. After this Markova and Dolin were not to dance with the Company until after World War II.

A new ballet was needed for the Van Damm seasons and in May 1935 a masterpiece was provided – de Valois' *The Rake's Progress.* Music by Gavin Gordon and designs by Rex Whistler matched the fine period quality of the choreography.

New male principals, Walter Gore and Harold Turner, both known from Ballet Rambert, created the Rake and the double role of the Dancing Master and Gentleman with a Rope, and Markova was the Betrayed Girl. The robust performances of Ursula Moreton, Sheila McCarthy, Gwyneth Mathews and Joy Newton reiterated the Company's demi-caractère ability.

(Left) Margot Fonteyn as solo dancer in 'Aïda' at Sadler's Wells. (Above) 'Rio Grande', left to right: Walter Gore as a Stevedore, Beatrice Appleyard as Queen of the Port, Margot Fonteyn as a Creole Girl, William Chappell as a Creole Boy. (Right, above) Leaflet for the Vic-Wells Ballet's first provincial tour in 1935. (Below) The Orgy Scene from 'The Rake's Progress', with Walter Gore, right, as the Rake, Ursula Moreton as the Dancer, William Chappell as the Rake's Friend. From left to right, Gwyneth Mathews, Elizabeth Miller, Pamela May, and Peggy Melliss as Ladies of the Town.

OPERA HOUSE
BLACKPOOL
Commencing WHIT-MONDAY, JUNE 10th
For Six Nights
Nightly at 7-45
Matinees: Whit-Monday and Saturday at 2-30
1935
VIVIAN VAN DAMM PRODUCTIONS LIMITED
By arrangement with
LILIAN BAYLIS, C.H., M.A., Oxon. (Hon.) LL.D. Birm. (Hon.)
present
THE
VIC-WELLS
BALLET
Under the direction of
NINETTE DE VALOIS
THE ENTIRE PRINCIPALS AND CORPS DE BALLET
FROM THE
OLD VIC AND SADLER'S WELLS THEATRES
LONDON
MARKOVA
and
ANTON DOLIN

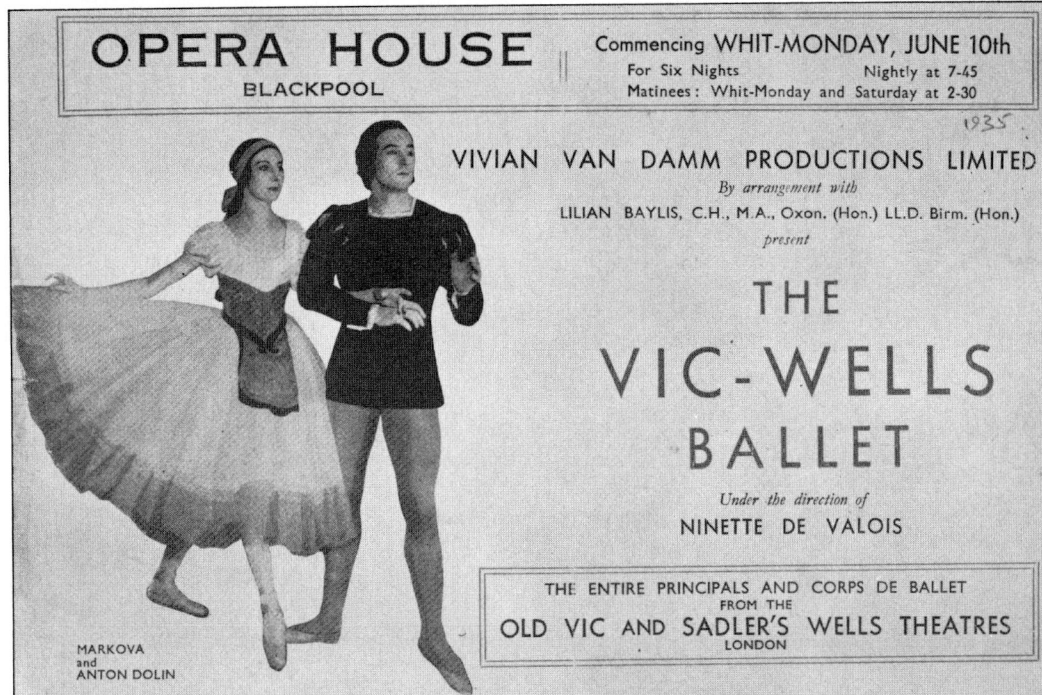

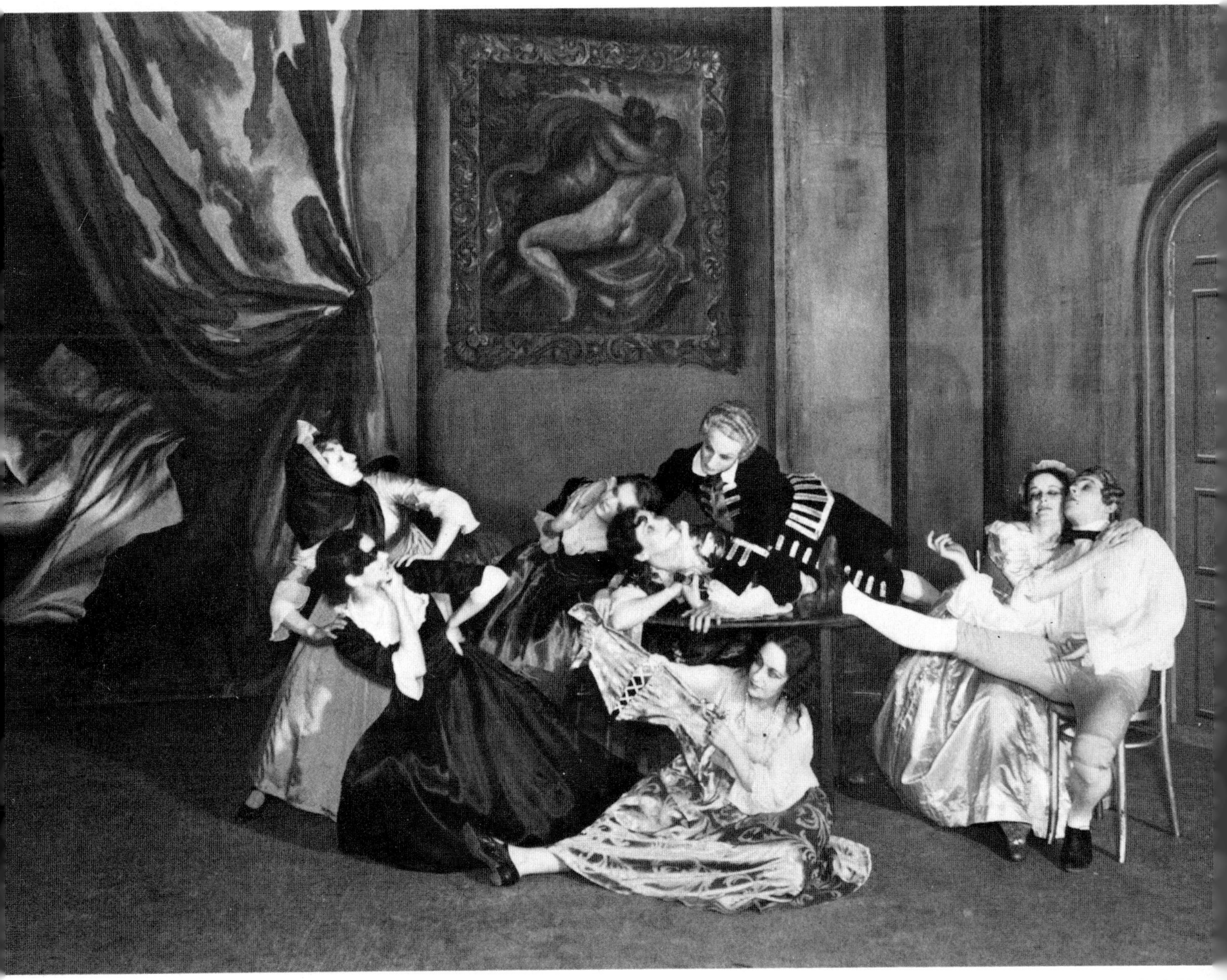

1935

One of Ashton's Camargo Society ballets joined the repertoire in October 1935. Anyone predicting the extent and length of its popularity might have been thought unduly optimistic, but *Façade*, in its various revisions, still enchants old and new audiences. William Walton had written the original orchestral suite to complement spoken poems by Edith Sitwell, and it was first given almost as a Sitwell family entertainment. Ashton matched and extended the musical jokes in his dances, and Rambert acquired the ballet from the Camargo Society.

In September 1935 Ashton joined the Vic-Wells Ballet as dancer and choreographer and staged *Façade* with one new number, the Country Dance. Ashton himself was the Dago and Fonteyn danced the impudent little Polka created by Markova. She was to be followed by countless delightful dancers but one

of the pertest and prettiest, in 1938, was 16-year-old Julia Farron.

Various leading dance schools gave, to chosen pupils, two-year scholarships to the Vic-Wells Ballet School, and Farron held the Cone School Scholarship. She first attracted attention in December 1935 in a special school revival of de Valois' *Nursery Suite*.

Another ballerina had joined the Company from Rambert, the exquisite Pearl Argyle. Ashton's next ballet, *Le Baiser de la Fée* (November 1935) gave her a perfect role as the enticing Fairy. Fonteyn was the demure Bride, and Turner, a brilliant technician, was the Young Man. He had trained with Alfred Haines in Manchester and later with Rambert and had danced at the Old Vic and with the Camargo Society. His work with the Vic-Wells in the thirties was of the greatest importance to British ballet.

'Façade'. (Right) Frederick Ashton as the Dago ; Julia Farron in the Polka ; (opposite, above) June Brae, Peggy Melliss, Pamela May and Beatrice Appleyard in the Waltz. (Below) 'Le Baiser de la Fée. Harold Turner as the Young Man, Margot Fonteyn as his Fiancée and Pearl Argyle as the Fairy.

(Overleaf) 'Apparitions', 1936, with Robert Helpmann as the Poet and Margot Fonteyn as the Woman in Balldress.

With *Apparitions* (February 1936) the Vic-Wells Ballet achieved a resounding success. Choreography by Ashton, structured to reveal the dramatic and lyrical qualities of Helpmann and Fonteyn, an evocative arrangement of Liszt by Lambert, and superb designs by Cecil Beaton made it a landmark work.

Ashton's range was subtly emphasised by the stylistically different romanticism of *Nocturne* (November 1936), with its Delius

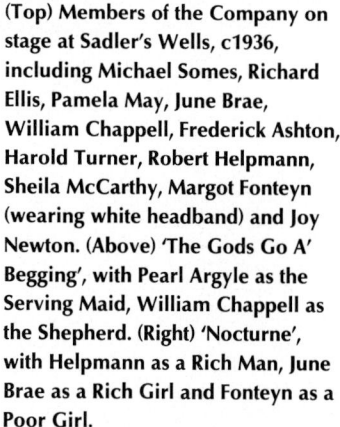

(Top) Members of the Company on stage at Sadler's Wells, c1936, including Michael Somes, Richard Ellis, Pamela May, June Brae, William Chappell, Frederick Ashton, Harold Turner, Robert Helpmann, Sheila McCarthy, Margot Fonteyn (wearing white headband) and Joy Newton. (Above) 'The Gods Go A' Begging', with Pearl Argyle as the Serving Maid, William Chappell as the Shepherd. (Right) 'Nocturne', with Helpmann as a Rich Man, June Brae as a Rich Girl and Fonteyn as a Poor Girl.

score and Sophie Fedorovitch designs.

One of the three ballets staged by de Valois in 1936, *The Gods Go A' Begging,* with Pearl Argyle as the Serving Maid and Chappell as the Shepherd, had a masterly light touch and a surprisingly durable quality in its Watteau-esque grace.

The Vic-Wells Company was now sufficiently well stocked with ballets and personalities to draw the public and to compete with visiting companies. Among its ballerinas, led by Fonteyn and Argyle, were the piquantly contrasted Pamela May and June Brae, and a new and delightful soubrette, Mary Honer. The men, dominated by the free-ranging talents of Helpmann, included Turner, Chappell, Ashton, the popular Leslie Edwards and Richard Ellis, and young hopefuls in Michael Somes and Alan Carter. With two remarkable choreographers and an outstanding music director, all the ingredients for an exciting future were present.

'A Wedding Bouquet'. (Top) Cartoon from The Sketch. (Above) Margot Fonteyn as Julia, Robert Helpmann as the Bridegroom, Mary Honer as the Bride, Julia Farron as Pepe. 'Les Patineurs'. (Left) Harold Turner as the Blue Skater, Mary Honer and Elizabeth Miller as the Blue Girls. (Opposite) June Brae as the Black Queen and Harold Turner as the Red Knight in 'Checkmate'.

1937 was a vintage year. Its three great successes, *Les Patineurs, A Wedding Bouquet* and *Checkmate,* are still in the repertoire. In each case the original cast has never been bettered.

In *Les Patineurs,* the smoothest possible blending of Meyerbeer arranged by Lambert, Chappell designs and Ashton's perfect tailoring of dance to his principals, resulted in a work that is perennially pleasing. Exciting technical tricks from Turner, Honer and Elizabeth Miller, smooth lyricism from Fonteyn and Helpmann and irresistible sparkle from May and Brae set the ballet's character.

In contrast, *A Wedding Bouquet* was eccentric and subtle. Words by Gertrude Stein, music and designs by Gerald (Lord) Berners, a chorus (later narrator) and a haphazard surrealistic action – all this either entranced or bored the viewer. Again, the casting was perfect : with Fonteyn as the wayward Julia, Brae as the tipsy Josephine, Honer as the wide-eyed Bride and Helpmann in his first major comedy role as an incomparable Bridegroom.

June 1937 saw the Company on its first overseas expedition, appearing at the Paris International Exhibition and staging de Valois' great *Checkmate.* Music specially composed by Arthur Bliss, designs by E. McKnight Kauffer in bold reds and blacks, made challenging collaborators for a typically forceful, thoughtful, intensely theatrical production. Brae was the epitome of evilly seductive power as the Black Queen, Turner had the memorable male lead as the Red Knight and Helpmann as the Red King gave the drama tragic conviction with his poignant study of senility.

Margot Fonteyn in some of her early roles. (Left) 'Giselle'. (Below, left) as Odette and Odile in 'Le Lac des Cygnes'. (Below, right) in 'Les Rendezvous'. (Opposite) 'Horoscope', with Fonteyn as the Young Woman, Michael Somes as the Young Man, and Alan Carter and Richard Ellis as the Gemini.

Markova would never be forgotten, but the Vic-Wells now had its own prima ballerina. Still very young, Fonteyn was meeting every challenge with the exciting qualities of the great artist. The child from Reigate by way of Shanghai was realising all de Valois' hopes. She danced her first *Giselle* (with Helpmann) on 19 January, 1937. *Le Lac des Cygnes* was a hurdle taken in two parts – she was never a natural exponent of virtuoso technical enchaînements. She danced Odette in December 1936, with Ruth French, a fine dancer who had been with Pavlova, as Odile; and in November 1938 she tackled the double role, again with Helpmann as Siegfried. Their partnership, which would delight audiences and become deservedly famous, was well on its way.

Another future partner emerged for Fonteyn when Ashton created *Horoscope* in January 1938. This ballet, to an original score by Lambert and with coolly beautiful designs by Sophie Fedorovitch, gave Somes his first great chance as the Young Man, and he proved to be a discovery of worth. May as the Moon, and Ellis and Carter as the Gemini, contributed to a production that heralded many superb pure-dance Ashton ballets.

1939

The great Tchaikovsky-Petipa production, *La Belle au Bois Dormant*, had dominated balletic thought ever since Diaghilev's historic and glorious failure with it in 1921. De Valois intended to stage it when she had a ballerina capable of dancing Aurora, and some essential alterations had made Sadler's Wells suitable for such an undertaking. Now the time was right. Nadia Benois produced traditional if dull designs, but Lambert adapted the score to excellent effect, and Sergeyev reproduced the Petipa choreography.

The Sleeping Princess was given a royal première, on 2 February, 1939 in the presence of Her Majesty Queen Mary. Fonteyn met everyone's idea of a youthful and joyous Aurora (she would enrich the part immeasurably over the years), Helpmann gave substance to the unrewarding role of the Prince, Brae was a radiant Lilac Fairy. Other memorable performances came from Honer and Turner in the Bluebird pas de deux, from May as the Diamond Fairy and Farron in the Breadcrumb (Finger) variation.

The ballet's success led to the Company's first gala appearance at Covent Garden. President Lebrun of France was on a State Visit and a Command Performance was arranged on 22 March, 1939. For the occasion a potted version was presented, made up of the Birthday and Wedding Acts. The Jewel Fairies in the Wedding were replaced by the fairy solos from the Prologue and the production was later televised by the BBC.

The 1939 production of 'The Sleeping Princess'. (Far left) Nicholas Sergeyev rehearsing Pamela May. (Below, left) Mary Honer and Harold Turner in the Blue Bird pas de deux. (Left) The Apotheosis, with Margot Fonteyn as Aurora, Robert Helpmann as Florimund, John Greenwood as Carabosse, and (on stairs) June Brae as the Lilac Fairy. (Below) The Fairies: back row, Julia Farron, June Brae, Palma Nye; front row, Mary Honer, Pamela May, Elizabeth Miller. (In margin) Programme designed by Rex Whistler for a Gala at the Royal Opera House on 22 March 1939.

1939–1940

(Right) Sophie Fedorovitch, designer of 'Dante Sonata'.
(Below) Scene from 'Dante Sonata'. The dancers include June Brae and Robert Helpmann as Children of Darkness, Michael Somes and Margot Fonteyn as Children of Light. The 1940 production of 'Coppélia'.
(Opposite, above) Mary Honer as Swanilda and Robert Helpmann as Franz ; (below) William Chappell, the designer.

1939, the year of *The Sleeping Princess,* also saw the outbreak of World War II. The Vic-Wells Ballet gave their last peacetime performance in Liverpool, on 2 September. War was declared the following day, and all plans had to be altered. A provincial tour was organised and the Company agreed to work on a cooperative financial basis. The 'phoney war' period allowed a return to Sadler's Wells on 26 December, 1939 and in January 1940 Ashton produced a passionate and purposeful work, *Dante Sonata,* a distillation of topical emotion, set to Liszt's sonata 'd'après une lecture de Dante'. It represented the struggle between Dark and Light and set Brae and Helpmann, as Children of Darkness, against Fonteyn, Somes and May as Children of Light. The action was greatly supported by superb lighting, and designs by Fedorovitch.

Fedorovitch, who had collaborated with Ashton from his early Rambert days, was an exceptional stage designer, notable for purity of colour and line and economy of effect. Her understanding of dancers in movement was evident in every costume, and she had a fine instinct for imaginative settings. Her accidental death in 1953 was a tragedy for ballet.

In spite of the escalating war, in April de Valois staged a new production of *Coppélia.* For the first time the third Act was included, reconstructed by Sergeyev from Petipa, and bold, colourful costumes and sets were designed by Chappell, soon to be in the Army. Swanilda was probably Honer's peak role, and she gave a sprightly and technically impeccable account of it. Helpmann was Franz, equally at home in the czardas as in the classical dancing. Claude Newman, a splendid character dancer and mime, was Dr Coppélius, a role which on Newman's call-up Helpmann would inherit and enlarge creatively.

1940

The most exciting and adventurous episode of the Company's entire story was the escape of the Sadler's Wells Ballet (as it was now called) from Holland in May 1940. They were there on a British Council cultural propaganda tour of neutral countries, but the neutrality of Holland was abruptly nullified by the German invasion on 10 May. This found the ballet just leaving Arnhem for The Hague, where for four days they waited, in the hope of a chance to leave. Eventually buses were found, and in groups, – quitting scenery, costumes, music and personal luggage – they were taken to Velsen and later Ijmuiden where a cargo boat brought them home.

The experience set the grimmer pattern of living and travelling in blitz-ridden London and the other bombed cities of Britain that would prevail for the rest of the war. The Company was faced with a constant need for adaptation in order to survive the many hardships which Britain was now suffering.

De Valois reacted to the disaster in Holland with an irresistible work, *The Prospect Before Us*, staged at Sadler's Wells on 4 July 1940. A tangled plot about rival 18th-century theatres gave no hint of the delightful dancing and characterisation. Naturally, with de Valois, it had a solid basis of period style and understanding, shared by the music (William Boyce arranged by Lambert) and the designs (Roger Furse inspired by Rowlandson). May as Mlle Théodore had a captivating role and there were countless clever portrait sketches (including an endearing trio of lawyers), all given point by the controlling comedy performance of Helpmann as the hilariously inebriated Mr O'Reilly.

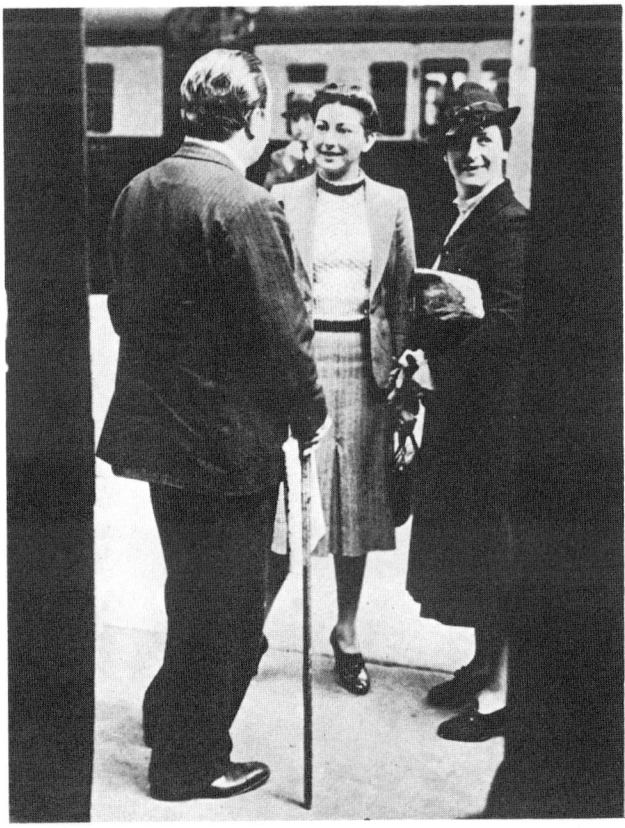

(Above) Members of the Company setting out for Holland in 1940; among them are de Valois, Palma Nye, Ashton, Fonteyn, Helpmann, May, Honer, Farron, Brae, Jill Gregory, Margaret Dale, Elizabeth Kennedy, John Hart, Deryk Mendel, Leslie Edwards, Claude Newman, Stanley Hall, and Moyra Fraser. The 'Prospect Before Us'. (Left, above) Robert Helpmann as the drunken Mr O'Reilly. (Below) Pamela May as Mlle Theodore and Alan Carter as Didelot. (Left) Setting out on a provincial tour in 1939. With Margot Fonteyn are Constant Lambert and Hilda Gaunt, who between 1939 and 1941 replaced the orchestra, playing two pianos.

1941

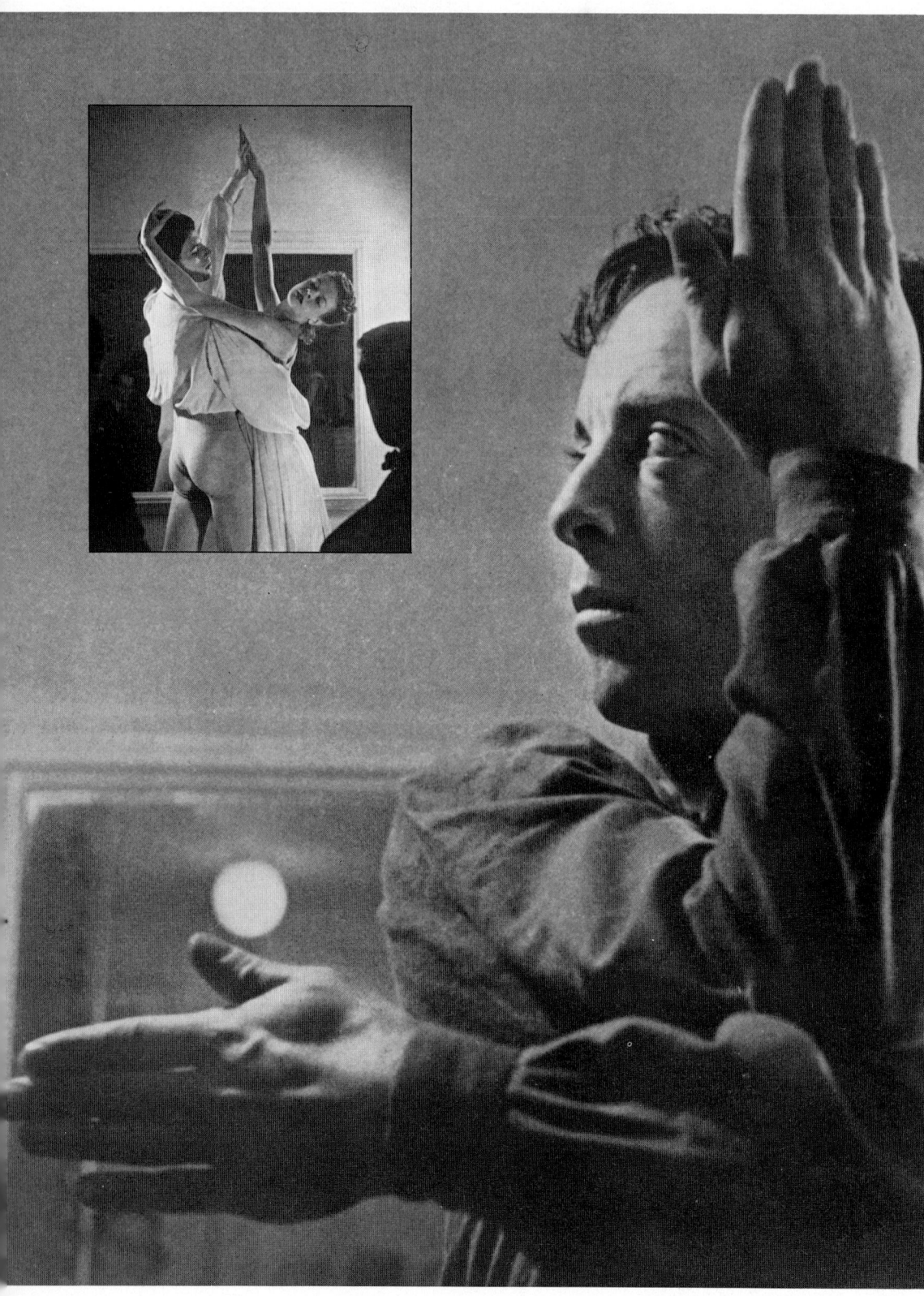

The bombing of London in September 1940 meant that Sadler's Wells was taken over by the authorities as a rest centre. The administrative headquarters of the Vic-Wells companies were moved to Burnley, but arrangements with Bronson Albery, manager of Wyndhams Theatres Ltd, enabled the ballet Company to open at the New (now Albery) Theatre in St Martin's Lane, in January 1941.

For London in wartime the New Theatre became synonymous with the Sadler's Wells Ballet. It was small, remarkably welcoming in atmosphere and had a record of drama triumphs. At first, music for the ballet was limited to two pianos, played by Hilda Gaunt and Lambert, and performances were only in daytime. Gradually an orchestra was restored and there were many different mutations of schedule, including at one time a midweek matinée and three performances on Saturdays – a gruelling work programme for principals and corps alike. Ashton and de Valois both staged new ballets in 1941. Ashton's *The Wanderer* (January) was an innovation for the Company : strikingly designed by Graham Sutherland, it was a pure dance work to Schubert's 'Wanderer Fantasie'. Acrobatic elements were introduced and it was sufficiently emotional to encourage audiences to invent their own names for the various characters. Helpmann, the Wanderer, was a compelling focal point for the other dancers : Young Love (May and Somes in a tenderly sensual duet), Wordly Glitter

'The Wanderer'. Robert Helpmann in the name part. (Inset) Michael Somes and Pamela May at the costume call with, silhouetted, Graham Sutherland reflected, left, and Frederick Ashton silhouetted, right.

(Fonteyn, unexpectedly steely), Compassion (Farron) and Children's Play (Margaret Dale and Deryk Mendel, two interesting new talents).

De Valois' ballet was *Orpheus and Eurydice* (May 1941), a mime ballet to offstage song. For many, this controlled, exquisitely designed (Fedorovitch) production, with Fonteyn (Love), Pamela May (Eurydice) and Helpmann (Orpheus) was a memorable pleasure. The charming country scene of the return to earth was led by Farron and a fine young dancer, John Hart, who would soon rank as a principal.

For the rest of the war, regular appearances in London would alternate with provincial tours and ENSA performances for the Forces. At the New Theatre or the Princes (now Shaftesbury) Theatre in 1944 the Company played to a closely knit, knowledgeable and loyal set of regulars willing to cope with increasingly difficult booking conditions – the leaflet listing forthcoming programmes was eventually covered in red and blue printed regulations about buying tickets – in order to keep in almost daily touch with performances.

In the provinces they were welcomed enthusiastically by general audiences. Children and pensioners saw them in the London parks from bandstand chairs at minimal prices, adoring the comedy of Fonteyn and Helpmann in the Tango in *Façade*, or the melting poetry of *Les Sylphides*. Servicemen and women, many from America, either in camp or on leave, became devotees of the Company.

'Orpheus and Eurydice'. (Above) Sketch from choreographic notes by de Valois and (below) the corresponding moment in the ballet, with Robert Helpmann as Orpheus.

1942

(Left, above) Costume call for 'Comus': Robert Helpmann with members of The Rout in masks designed by Oliver Messel.
(Left) 'The Birds', with Moyra Fraser as the Hen and Margaret Dale and Joan Sheldon as Sparrows.

(Above) 'Hamlet', with Robert Helpmann as Hamlet, David Paltenghi as Claudius, and Celia Franca as Gertrude.

The conscription of male dancers into the armed forces went on, and Ashton was drafted into the RAF in June 1941. Somes, Edwards, Carter and Richard Ellis had left. Helpmann, rightly considered to be a key figure in the Company's survival, was exempted. Hart, for the short time left him before call-up, shared many of the leading roles, making a particular success of *Les Sylphides* and the Bluebird pas de deux. New recruits were Alexis Rassine, David Paltenghi, Leo Kersley and Gordon Hamilton.

Helpmann, whose performing life had embraced acting as well as dancing, now embarked on choreography, with three ballets in a year. The first, *Comus* (January 1942) acknowledged its Masque origin in Oliver Messel's designs, influenced by Inigo Jones; in the Lambert-arranged Purcell score; and in the use of the spoken word. Its civilised and fluent action countered wartime austerity. *Hamlet* (May 1942) was a triumph in its tautly regulated, deeply considered translation of the play into a surrealist dream. Helpmann discovered the ideal designer in the painter Leslie Hurry, and the Tchaikovsky Fantasy Overture might have been specially composed for the ballet.

The Birds (November) differed in style from its predecessors. It was a gentle comedy, classically based, giving Beryl Grey her first created role as the Nightingale with Rassine as the Dove. Moyra Fraser, whose elegant long line had been displayed as Sabrina in *Comus*, now proved her clowning propensities as the Hen. Like *Comus* and *Hamlet*, *The Birds* was a unity of arts, with ravishing designs by Chiang Yee and music by Respighi.

1943

(Above) HRH The Princess Elizabeth (now Queen Elizabeth II), HRH The Princess Margaret and HM Queen Elizabeth (now Queen Elizabeth The Queen Mother) at a performance of 'The Quest', 1943. The Royal Family has always maintained a close interest in the Company's work, and Princess Margaret has been its President since 1956. (Below) 'The Quest'. Moira Shearer as Pride with: standing, Anthony Burke as Lechery, Nigel Desmond as Sloth; seated, Ray Powell as Gluttony and Gordon Hamilton as Avarice.
(Opposite) 'Le Lac des Cygnes', above, Margot Fonteyn and Robert Helpmann; below, Beryl Grey as Odette.

Ashton was given leave in 1943 to mount a new ballet and he chose to stage *The Quest* (April) based on Spenser's *The Faerie Queene*. A commissioned score from William Walton and designs by John Piper should have ensured success. Its narrative strength, however, failed, in spite of a clever set of solos for the Seven Deadly Sins led by a beautiful new red-haired dancer, Moira Shearer, as Pride, and of an alluringly sinuous role for Grey as the false Duessa. Fonteyn as Una and Helpmann as St George had all-too-predictable roles.

The Company continued to dance with the passionate involve-ment that danger and privation tend to inspire. Now they em-barked (September 1943) on a full-scale revision of *Le Lac des Cygnes*, staged again by Sergeyev

and designed with magnificent imagination and coherence by Leslie Hurry. None of his later reconsidered versions of the ballet equalled this first fresh encounter with it. Fonteyn and Helpmann danced it with committed and deeply moving intensity. They shared the leads with Grey and Paltenghi, a handsome cavalier if a limited dancer. Grey had made her début as Odette-Odile on 11 June 1942, her fifteenth birthday, giving an excitingly accomplished interpretation.

In the pas de trois, Rassine was joined by a delightful pair of soloists, Margaret Dale and Joan Sheldon. Dale, remembered for a high all-round standard of performance, later achieved ballerina status in *Coppélia* at Covent Garden before making a career in dance television as a producer.

1943–1944

The Sadler's Wells Ballet was now widely loved and its value to the war effort established. Although not a large Company, it was an important one: an integrated team of individuals of a high technical standard and great dramatic ability. Thorough professionals, they adapted to every kind of performing demand. Dancing in the open air in London parks or in garrison theatres demanded a different approach from dancing in regular theatres with orthodox lighting and staging conditions.

At the Princes Theatre in October 1944 another major Helpmann ballet, with a scenario by Michael Benthall, was premièred, *Miracle in the Gorbals*. This modern-dress drama, of a Stranger who brings a suicide back to life and is killed by a gang of toughs, was controversial in theme but splendidly convincing in performance. Edward Burra was the ideal choice of designer to bring the Glasgow slum and shipyard ambiance to life, and Bliss composed an effective score. Helpmann drew on El Greco paintings for groupings and hand movements and created the central role with restrained power. Pauline Clayden and Celia Franca gave fine portrayals of the Suicide and the Prostitute, and the ballet was notable for satisfying cameos such as Leslie Edwards' perfectly conceived Beggar.

(Above) Cartoon from The Tatler, showing Fonteyn and Helpmann in the tango from 'Façade'. (Below, left) 'Les Sylphides' performed in Victoria Park, East London, 1943. (Below, right) Robert Helpmann as Dr Coppélius, a role which he first danced in 1941. 'Promenade', 1943, (choreography by de Valois). Gordon Hamilton as the Lepidopterist with Moira Shearer, Alexis Rassine and Ray Powell.

(Right) Margot Fonteyn and Robert Helpmann on tour with ENSA in 1945. (Below) 'Miracle in the Gorbals': left, Moira Shearer and Alexis Rassine as the Lovers, with Jean Bedells; right, the final scene, with Helpmann as the Stranger, Leslie Edwards as a Beggar, Celia Franca as the Prostitute and Pauline Clayden as the Suicide.

1946

Victory over Hitler in May 1945 was marked by a celebratory *Coppélia*, and victory over Japan came during a brief return to Sadler's Wells later that year. The future was already planned. The Royal Opera House, Covent Garden, would reopen on 20 February 1946 with a new production of *The Sleeping Beauty* by the Sadler's Wells Ballet.

Every effort was directed towards the great day. Messel completed a set of designs that as a whole have never been surpassed. Their gradual erosion and final abandonment was no doubt inevitable but in the beginning they seemed the essence of fairy tale enchantment. The choreographic content was spruced up and a few alterations and additions made. The Company was of course augmented for the Opera House stage. A long series of performances was scheduled with alternating casts: Fonteyn and Helpmann (Helpmann doubling as Carabosse), May and Shearer both dancing with Paltenghi. Grey, later to dance Aurora, was the first Lilac Fairy, gracious in manner and impressively accurate in her solo.

On the opening night, May and Rassine danced the Bluebird pas de deux. The second night introduced to London Bolshoi-trained Violetta Prokhorova (she later used her married name of Elvin) whose totally different style and flexible Russian back were sensational. Somes danced the Florestan pas de trois with Shearer and Gerd Larsen, who had joined the Company in 1944. Turner, who had come back from the forces in April 1945, led the Three Ivans, and alternated as Bluebird with Rassine. New names of importance among the fairies were Gillian Lynne and Anne Negus.

The première was a Royal Gala, the first of many such festive postwar occasions at the Opera House.

The 1946 production of 'The Sleeping Beauty', with décor by Oliver Messel. (Right) Act I, Beryl Grey as The Lilac Fairy, with the other Fairies: Gerd Larsen, Gillian Lynne, Anne Negus, Pauline Clayden and Margaret Dale; Robert Helpmann as Carabosse. (Below, left) Margot Fonteyn as Princess Aurora, Robert Helpmann as Prince Florimund. (Below, right) Pamela May as Princess Aurora. (Opposite, below left) Moira Shearer as Aurora, David Paltenghi as Florimund; below right, Violetta Prokhorova with Alexis Rassine in the Bluebird pas de deux.

1946

Adapting to conditions at Covent Garden took time, and the greatest success of the first year – one that has proved a classic of our time – was Ashton's *Symphonic Variations*. The César Franck score drew from him the most varied and fluent choreography that he had yet sustained, and Fedorovitch contributed inspired simplicity in the designs. The sextet of dancers, Fonteyn and Somes, May, Shearer, Henry Danton and a fine young classicist, Brian Shaw, set an unbeatable standard in concerted performance.

More important for the future, however, was the opening of a second company at Sadler's Wells. The Sadler's Wells Opera (later Theatre) Ballet, which gave its first performance on 8 April 1946 would prove the source from which the mainstream of performing and creative talent would flow. Its early programmes showed ballets by Andrée Howard, a rare and undervalued choreographer from Rambert, and by Celia Franca, Anthony Burke and Alan Carter, all well-known dancers with the Sadler's Wells Ballet. Brae, Franca, Leo Kersley and Alan Carter led the Company, soon joined by new names : sixteen-year-old Anne Heaton, Nadia Nerina (Moore) and Donald Britton.

The Company's overall director was de Valois, with Ursula Moreton as her assistant. The Ballet Mistress was Peggy Van Praagh, who earlier had been with Rambert and Antony Tudor's London Ballet, and who had joined the Sadler's Wells Ballet in 1941 as dancer and teacher.

(Opposite) 'Symphonic Variations', with Margot Fonteyn, Brian Shaw, Michael Somes, Pamela May, Moira Shearer, Henry Danton. (Left) 'Assembly Ball', 1946, Andrée Howard's first ballet for Sadler's Wells Theatre Ballet. Leo Kersley as Master of Ceremonies, June Brae as the Lady. (Below) 'Mardi Gras' Andrée Howard's second creation for the Theatre Ballet. Left, Anne Heaton as the Girl; right Nadia Nerina as a Circus Dancer, Leo Kersley as a Reveller in White; centre Donald Britton as a Boy, John Cranko as a Pugilist.

1947

(Right) 'The Three-Cornered Hat'.
Léonide Massine as the Miller and
Violetta Elvin as the Miller's Wife.
(Below) 'Mam'zelle Angot', with
Margot Fonteyn as the heroine,
Alexander Grant as the Barber.
(Opposite) 'La Boutique Fantasque',
with Alexis Rassine as the Snob,
Franklin White as the Melon
Hawker.

Léonide Massine had dominated the later Diaghilev and post-Diaghilev period as choreographer and dancer. His variety of composition from demi-caractère comedy to symphonic ballet, and his charismatic personality brought him enthusiastic admirers. He had been last seen in England in 1938 and spent the war years in America. Now, in February 1947, he returned to stage some of his ballets at Covent Garden.

Two from his Diaghilev repertoire, The Three-Cornered Hat and La Boutique Fantasque, were revived with great care, and the splendid designs, by Picasso and André Derain respectively, looked fresh and attractive. Massine himself danced the Miller in The Three-Cornered Hat with magnetic force.

Fonteyn and Elvin alternated as the Miller's Wife, and Hart identified completely with the Corregidor. The dancers were less at home with Boutique although clever characterisations – particularly Rassine's Snob – emerged. Neither Shearer nor May could sparkle sufficiently as the Can-Can Dancer.

Mam'zelle Angot (November 1947) was a newer work, created for Ballet Theatre in America in 1943. Massine revised it without making it completely viable and Derain designed it charmingly. The outstanding performance came from Alexander Grant, a New Zealander, as the Barber. The title role was taken by Fonteyn, followed by Julia Farron and a notably sure technician, the attractive Avril Navarre.

1947

Sadler's Wells Theatre Ballet was settling into its stride, with some promising new dancers supporting the established names. There was a strong South African contingent. As well as Nadia Nerina and John Cranko, these included Patricia Miller, David Poole, Pamela Chrimes and Maryon Lane. Anne Heaton and Nerina had been joined as potential ballerinas by Elaine Fifield from Australia. Donald Britton, Michael Boulton and Michael Hogan were dancing leads, as well as Hans Zullig from Ballets Jooss.

Cranko, Kenneth MacMillan and Peter Darrell were all to have notable careers in choreography and directorship. Stanley Holden was proving, in roles like the Witch in Andrée Howard's delectable send-up of the Romantic Era, *Selina* (November 1948), that he was a great comedy dancer.

Selina was the last ballet staged for them by Andrée Howard. Like her other works for the Company it has vanished, but one of her masterpieces, *La Fête Etrange*, revived in 1947 and performed exquisitely by June Brae, Donald Britton and Anthony Burke, survives in the repertoire.

As well as established choreographers like Ashton, who created *Valses Nobles et Sentimentales* for them in October 1947, and Andrée Howard, the Theatre Ballet were performing, to the enjoyment of their audiences, works by Company members. By 1948 Cranko had staged *Adieu*, *Tritsch-Tratsch* and *Children's Corner*, all mounted originally for the University of Cape Town Ballet. Franca had been an early contributor with *Khadra* (May 1946). Burke's *The Vagabonds* (October 1946) was a well-constructed drama and Alan Carter's lively *The Catch* a popular peasant trio.

(Above) June Brae as the Bride, Donald Britton as a Country Boy and Anthony Burke as the Bridegroom in 'La Fête Etrange'. (Left) 'Valses Nobles et Sentimentales', with Anne Heaton and Peter Darrell, Kenneth MacMillan, Donald Britton, Michael Hogan, and Michael Boulton; (right) Hans Zullig as Simplice, a Poet, Stanley Holden as Agnes, a Witch, and David Gill as Lord Ravensgarth in 'Selina'.

At Covent Garden Ashton was preparing *Cinderella,* the first full-length ballet to be composed by a British choreographer, (December 1948). It used the Prokofiev score and had designs by Jean-Denis Malclès (superseded in 1965 by Henry Bardon and David Walker). Full-length ballets had been considered old-fashioned in Western Europe since Diaghilev and Fokine. The wheel was beginning to turn. In Fonteyn's absence through injury, Shearer, now widely known through the film *The Red Shoes,* created the title role, sharing it with Elvin. The saving grace, theatrically speaking, of an agreeable but thinly spread evening was the partnership of Ashton and Helpmann as the irrepressible Ugly Sisters – comic performances that would become richly embellished over the years and make successors despair.

In February Ashton had composed a finer ballet, *Scènes de Ballet.* An entirely satisfying work, created by Fonteyn and Somes, it was ahead of its time and only reached its peak many years later with Antoinette Sibley.

The old repertoire was struggling to find its feet in the new surroundings. *Checkmate* (November 1947) had gone well and in May 1948 *Job* was staged with designs by John Piper, still based on Blake and distinguished by warmly modulated ranges of colour. Helpmann, who was acting Hamlet and other principal roles at the Shakespeare Memorial Theatre, returned as a superbly challenging Satan.

(Left) John Piper's setting for 'Job' with Robert Helpmann as Satan. (Right, above) Margot Fonteyn and Michael Somes in 'Scènes de Ballet', in the original setting by André Beaurepaire. (Right, below) Moira Shearer and Michael Somes in 'Cinderella'.

THE BRITISH CAPTURE NEW YORK

Even those in the dance world who knew the Sadler's Wells Ballet before it came here and were certain of its success in New York would not have ventured to predict as complete a triumph as the company is having at this writing, midway in its four-week season at the Metropolitan Opera House. Nor could they foresee the sincere and over-whelming welcome New York has accorded the company.

This is TIME's Issue of November 14, 1949

New York Metropolitan Opera House

See Page 28

ATLANTIC OVERSEAS EDITION

TIME

THE WEEKLY NEWSMAGAZINE

BALLERINA MARGOT FONTEYN
For Sleeping Beauty, an awakened audience.

First to arrive from London were Leslie Edwards, David Webster (general manager), Robert Helpmann, Frederick Ashton and Margot Fonteyn. Nora Kaye (next to Helpmann) and S. Hurok (extreme right) met them at the airport. (Photo Walter E. Owen)

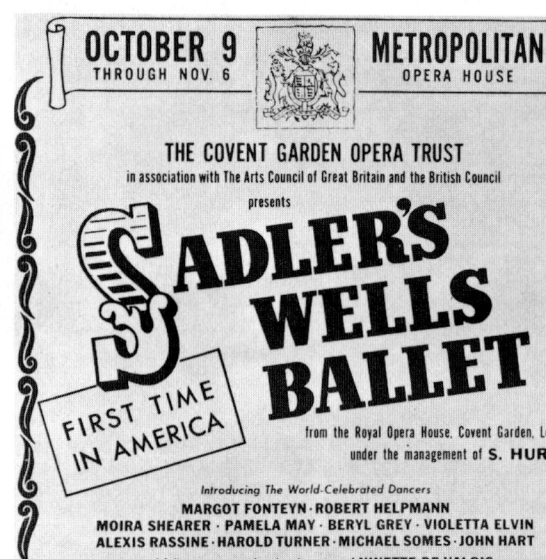

AFTER THE PHENOMENAL DOLLAR-EARNING SUCCESS OF THE SADLER'S WELLS BALLET IN NEW YORK, THE CABINET IS CONTEMPLATING ANOTHER MISSION TO AMERICA.

VICKY

Discussions between Sol Hurok, the great American impresario, and David Webster, General Administrator of The Royal Opera House, resulted in an engagement for the Sadler's Wells Ballet to appear at the Metropolitan Opera House, New York, for a season opening 9 October 1949.

The date became a famous victory for the Company that de Valois had started with six dancers at the Old Vic. The chosen ballet was *The Sleeping Beauty*, led of course by Fonteyn and Helpmann, with Grey as the Lilac Fairy and Shearer and Rassine in the Bluebird pas de deux. Fonteyn's personal triumph was tremendous and the confidence it engendered carried her forward to her eventual title of prima ballerina assoluta. All the same, it was the magnitude of the production, the beauty of the designs, and the wealth of fine classical choreography, danced with impeccable British musicality and precision, that made New York audiences their friends for life.

The season was followed by a two-months' tour that included Philadelphia and Chicago, Toronto, Ottawa and Montreal. The role of the Company as cultural ambassadors and revenue raisers for Britain was emphasised in its reception home by the Chancellor of the Exchequer, Sir Stafford Cripps.

This initial sally across the Atlantic was the first of many, and the beginning of an extraordinary relationship between the British company and the growing number of balletgoers in the United States. Critics and public earmarked their favourites among dancers and ballets, often reacting differently from their English counterparts. Their feelings of involvement can be recognised by the establishment in 1972 of 'The American Friends of Covent Garden and The Royal Ballet Inc', an organisation that, like the Friends of Covent Garden in London, has even on occasion contributed funds towards productions.

(Opposite, above) Arrival in New York. (Opposite, left) Cover of Time Magazine, 14 November 1949. (Centre) Advertisement from Dance News. (Below) Cartoon by Vicky from the News Chronicle. (Above, left) Photo from The Sketch showing Margot Fonteyn being fitted for a suit by Michael Sherard ; for the trip to New York all ballerinas were supplied with clothes made by British fashion houses. (Above, right) Margot Fonteyn and Robert Helpmann signing autographs at the stage door of the Metropolitan Opera House after the opening night, 9 October 1949.

1950–1951

The excitement of success across the Atlantic may have contributed in May 1950 to an odd mistake: the Company celebrated the 21st anniversary of the re-opening of Sadler's Wells a year too early. It was a good evening, however, involving both companies, calling in retired talent for a riotous Orgy Scene from *Rake*, and producing de Valois' final appearance as a dancer in her created role of Webster in *A Wedding Bouquet*. She had also just staged her last ballet. *Don Quixote* (February), to a score by Roberto Gerhard and with imaginative designs by Burra, was a mature, concise and theatrically memorable production that failed to appeal to press and public.

The contact with the United States resulted in the Company's first Balanchine revival, *Ballet Imperial* (April 1950). Its performance was valiant rather than brilliant, by dancers unused to Balanchine's style. The most at ease was Grey, in the pas de trois with John Field and Kenneth MacMillan.

Another successful tour in 1950/51 took the dancers to California where in November 1950 Helpmann ended an immensely valuable eighteen-year connection with the Company. 1951 found them in Chicago, and in the New Year Honours de Valois was created a Dame of the British Empire.

In July 1951 Lambert's last composition, *Tiresias*, was staged with choreography by Ashton. The collaboration, for once, did not work well. The ballet was not only disliked by the press but was made the occasion of severe criticism levelled at the artistic management of Covent Garden. A month later, still deeply distressed at the reaction, Lambert died of diabetes.

Ashton, however, had a conditional success, as far as the difficult scenario allowed, with *Daphnis and Chloë* (April 1951). The Greek designs by John Craxton helped it considerably, and Fonteyn was marvellously moving as the captured and threatened Chloë.

Sadler's Wells Theatre Ballet meanwhile had resiliently weathered a disaster: in June 1949 the Theatre Royal, Hanley, had burnt down, together with much of the Company's scenery and costumes. In May 1949 they had staged *Le Lac des Cygnes Act II*, with Elaine Fifield as the Swan Queen. Soon Svetlana Beriosova, who joined the Company in May 1950, was dancing Odette with exciting classical potential.

(Above, left) Twenty-first birthday celebrations at Sadler's Wells in May 1950, with Ninette de Valois, Mary Honer, Ursula Moreton, Constant Lambert, Julia Farron, Ailne Phillips, Robert Irving (conductor), Molly Brown and Sheila McCarthy. (Below, left) Beryl Grey, Kenneth MacMillan and John Field in 'Ballet Imperial'. (Below, right) Margot Fonteyn as Chloë in 'Daphnis and Chloë. (Above) Sadlers Wells Theatre Ballet production of 'Le Lac des Cygnes', Act II. Svetlana Beriosova as Odette, Michael Hogan as Prince Siegfried, Peter Wright as Benno.

(Opposite, below) Donald Britton as Franz, Elaine Fifield as Swanilda, in 'Coppélia'. (Opposite, above) Johaar Mosaval as Jasper in 'Pineapple Poll', which he first danced in 1952. (Above) Scene from 'Pineapple Poll'. Centre, Elaine Fifield as Poll, David Poole as Jasper, Sheilah O'Reilly as Mrs Dimple, David Blair as Captain Belaye, Stella Claire as Blanche. (Right) Sol Hurok's advertisement for the Theatre Ballet's tour of the United States.

It was now the turn of Sadler's Wells Theatre Ballet to visit America. Their tour lasted from October 1951 to April 1952 and took them on an extensive itinerary throughout the States and Canada. It was a strenuous programme for a young company, but they were guided by van Praagh and exhilarated by their appreciative audiences. Their repertoire included two classics staged earlier that year: *Coppélia,* designed by Loudon Sainthill and danced by Fifield and David Blair, and a two-act *Casse-Noisette* (The Kingdom of Snow and The Kingdom of Sweets) staged by Ashton and designed by Beaton, in which

Beriosova was the Snow Queen and Fifield the Sugar Plum Fairy.

Among their own ballets they had their latest hit, Cranko's *Pineapple Poll* (March 1951), one of the most popular works ever choreographed for them. Based on one of W. S. Gilbert's 'Bab Ballads', it was set to a clever pot-pourri of Sullivan melodies arranged by Charles Mackerras and brilliantly designed by Osbert Lancaster. Again, the first cast of Fifield as Poll, Blair as the ladykiller Captain Belaye, and Poole as the potboy Jasper could not be surpassed, but the three roles have since had many fine interpreters. One of them, Johaar Mosaval,

played Jasper 310 times in the United Kingdom alone, making the record number of performances in any role by a member of The Royal Ballet.

Cranko's ability as a comedy choreographer was fully established by this first major work, although his talent in other directions had been proved in the well-constructed *Sea Change* and the sensitive *Beauty and the Beast* (both in 1949). May 1951 had also seen a unusual and sadly lost ballet from him, *Harlequin in April,* an artistically harmonious production with an Arts Council-commissioned score by Richard Arnell and designs by John Piper.

At Covent Garden the early fifties brought something of a recession as far as new works were concerned. Ashton choreographed a full-length *Sylvia* (September 1952) which had some enjoyable and amusing scenes. Fonteyn, and later Grey, Elvin and Nerina, danced the difficult leading role. Somes was Aminta, and one of the best performances came from Hart as Orion.

The main Company was drawing now on the top line of the Sadler's Wells Theatre Ballet. By the mid-fifties Nerina, Beriosova, Heaton, Fifield and Blair were all based on Covent Garden. Nerina was one of the ballerinas in Ashton's charming pièce d'occasion, *Homage to the Queen*, premièred on Coronation Night, 2 June 1953, and she and Blair danced *Coppélia* in a new production designed by Osbert Lancaster (March 1954).

The Company had completed their third North American tour. They had taken with them a new production of *Le Lac des Cygnes* premièred in December 1952 with Grey and Field, now an exciting partnership. For this there were revised sets and costumes by Hurry, and a popular choreographic addition was Ashton's Neapolitan Dance for Farron and Grant.

For the Edinburgh Festival (August 1954) the Company invited the Russian régisseur Serge Grigoriev and his wife Lubov Tchernicheva to stage Fokine's *The Firebird*. Fonteyn, dancing the lead, was coached by the role's creator, Tamara Karsavina. Somes, Ashton and Beriosova completed a remarkable opening quartet of principals.

(Opposite) 'Homage to the Queen'. Margot Fonteyn with, at centre, Violetta Elvin, Beryl Grey, Nadia Nerina ; at side, left to right, Brian Shaw, Rowena Jackson, Philip Chatfield, Svetlana Beriosova, Rosemary Lindsay, Bryan Ashbridge, Julia Farron and Alexander Grant. (Left) 'Sylvia', with Fonteyn as Sylvia, John Hart as Orion and Brian Shaw as the Slave. (Below, left) Margot Fonteyn in 'The Firebird'. (Below, right) Nadia Nerina as Swanilda, David Blair as Franz in the 1954 'Coppélia'.

In 1953 Sadler's Wells Theatre Ballet was developing a new group of leading dancers. They continued to experiment with choreographic talent, and MacMillan staged his first ballet, *Somnambulism*, for the Sadler's Wells Choreographic Group in February 1953. Alfred Rodrigues, a dancer with the Covent Garden Company, mounted an interesting work, *Blood Wedding* (June 1953), for the Theatre Ballet. A specially composed score by Dennis Aplvor and sultry designs by Isabel Lambert contributed to an exciting action based on Garcia Lorca's play, 'Bodas de Sangre'. Fifield was the Bride, and Pirmin Trecu the Bridegroom; Trecu, a Basque who had graduated from the School to the Company in 1947, had the dual ability of making his mark in the classical repertoire and dancing in some effective Spanish divertissements such as *El Destino* (1950).

Cranko's next success was *The Lady and the Fool* (February 1954). Later transferred to Covent Garden, it was an unashamedly sentimental tale of a Society beauty who fell in love with a Clown; but the expertly characterised dances and the touching central theme of the tall and the short clowns were unfailingly theatrical. MacMillan and Mosaval as the Clowns, Patricia Miller as La Capricciosa and the trio of suitors, David Poole, David Gill and Peter Wright (who would one day direct the Touring Company) made the early performances outstandingly entertaining.

(Left) Kenneth MacMillan as Moondog, Johaar Mosaval as Bootface in 'The Lady and the Fool'. (Above) Rehearsal of 'The Lady and the Fool', with Peter Wright, David Poole, David Gill and Patricia Miller. (Below) Pirmin Trecu as the Bridegroom and David Poole as Leonardo in 'Blood Wedding'.

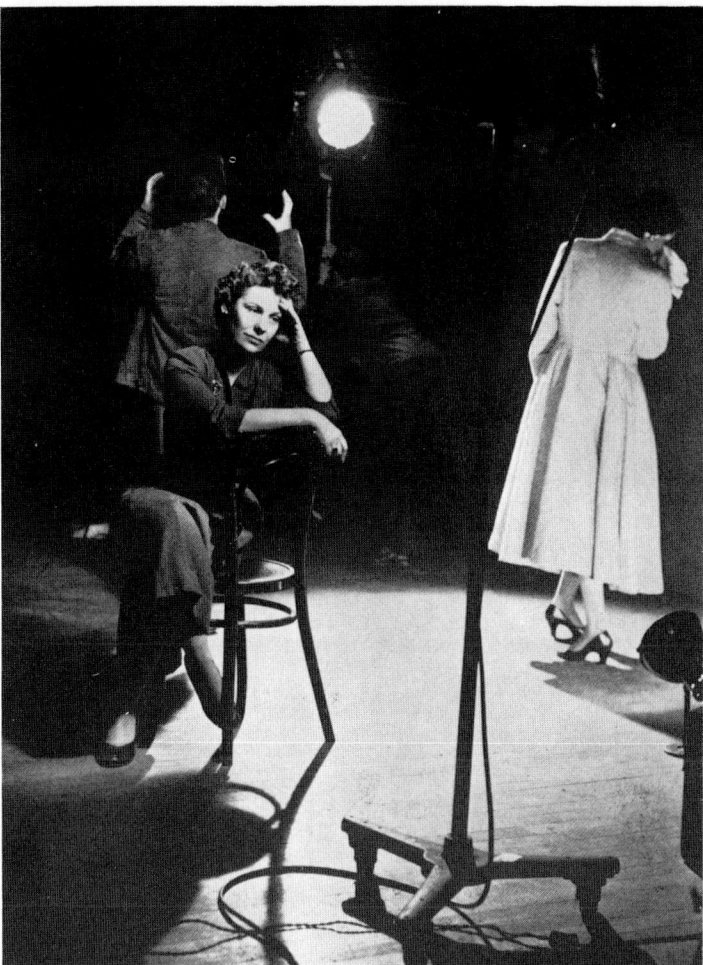

MacMillan's first ballet for Sadler's Wells Theatre Ballet, Stravinsky's *Danses Concertantes* (January 1955), displayed immediately a unique style of dance invention and a remarkably firm control. He gave dancers new challenges and discovered the talents likely to suit his work. Maryon Lane was admirable both in this ballet and four months later in *House of Birds*. Margaret Hill brought a poignant charm to the leading role of *Solitaire* (June 1956), a singularly fresh and youthful work with music by Malcolm Arnold and evocative designs by Desmond Heeley.

In June and July 1954 the Theatre Ballet fulfilled engagements in South Africa where, in Johannesburg, they premièred a clever comedy, *Café des Sports*, by Rodrigues. Maryon Lane was an enticing Urchin; Poole and the delightful young Annette Page were amusing as Essential Artists.

The dancers and choreographers of the Theatre Ballet owed much to Peggy van Praagh, Assistant Director (to de Valois) from 1951 to 1955. Her ability to give patient and concerned attention to the development of talent was exceptional.

(Left, above) 'Danses Concertantes', with Maryon Lane and, from left, David Poole, Gilbert Vernon, Bryan Lawrence, Donald MacLeary, Donald Britton; (below) Anne Heaton in 'Giselle', 1956, with Henry Legerton as Hilarion. (Centre) 'Solitaire'. Back row right to left: Margaret Hill, Sara Neil, Michael Boulton, Donald MacLeary, Donald Britton. (Above) Peggy van Praagh on stage at Sadler's Wells Theatre.

1956

Through 1956 and 1957 new productions at Covent Garden remained disappointing. Ashton was weathering a difficult creative period, but a pièce d'occasion for the Company's 25th Birthday, *Birthday Offering* (May 1956), drew from him felicities of dance for seven ballerinas (Fonteyn, Grey, Elvin, Nerina, Beriosova, Fifield and Rowena Jackson). MacMillan had staged *Noctambules* (March 1956); Rodrigues had staged *The Miraculous Mandarin* (August 1956); and in January 1957 Cranko was given an over-testing assignment in a full-length score by Benjamin Britten, *The Prince of the Pagodas*. None of them was at his best, and the interest of these years lay in the development of dancers.

The new generation, however, were unlucky in the short-lived vehicles created for them. Heaton had *A Mirror for Witches* (Andrée Howard 1952); Fifield, *Madame Chrysanthème* (Ashton 1955); Beriosova, *Rinaldo and Armida* (Ashton 1955) and *The Prince of the Pagodas*. Fortunately most of them also danced the classics, as did Rowena Jackson, Anya Linden and Rosemary Lindsay. There were good danseurs nobles in Field, Philip Chatfield and Desmond Doyle, and the demi-caractère tradition was stalwartly upheld by Alexander Grant and Ray Powell.

(Opposite, left) 'Birthday Offering'. At centre, Margot Fonteyn and Michael Somes; left to right, Elaine Fifield, Brian Shaw, Rowena Jackson, Desmond Doyle, Svetlana Beriosova, Bryan Ashbridge, Beryl Grey, Philip Chatfield, Violetta Elvin, David Blair, Nadia Nerina and Alexander Grant; (below) Brian Shaw in the Bluebird pas de deux, which he first danced in 1956.

(Left) David Blair, Benjamin Britten, Svetlana Beriosova and John Cranko after the première of 'The Prince of the Pagodas' on 1 January 1957. (Below) Beriosova as Princess Belle Rose and Blair as the Prince of the Pagodas.

1957

(Right) Poster advertising for the first time the Company's 'Royal' status, on 26 March 1957. (Below) Margot Fonteyn as the Ballerina and Peter Clegg as the Blackamoor in 'Petrushka'. (Inset) Frederick Ashton, in costume as the Charlatan, with Lubov Tchernicheva and Serge Grigoriev.

On 31 October 1956 Queen Elizabeth II granted a Charter to the Sadler's Wells Ballet authorising them to be called in future The Royal Ballet. Both Companies shared the title. The larger group continued to perform primarily at Covent Garden; the smaller Touring Company was now directed by John Field.

The first major venture at Covent Garden was *The Prince of the Pagodas*, much-heralded and sadly disappointing, and in March, encouraged by the success of *The Firebird*, they asked Grigoriev and Tchernicheva to stage *Petrushka*. Great pains were taken over it, and the first cast of Fonteyn as The Doll, Grant as Petrushka, and Peter Clegg, one of their best young character dancers, as The Blackamoor, was meticulously rehearsed. What was missing, and remained so in later years, was the Russian zest and understanding that had made the masterwork effective.

Meanwhile the Touring Company, appearing at Covent Garden in January 1958, mounted a significant ballet, MacMillan's *The Burrow*. Freely based on the type of situation immortalised by 'The Diary of Anne Frank', its emphasis on neuroses made it a forerunner of other MacMillan productions. The music was by Frank Martin and, as with *Noctambules*, the designer was Nicholas Georgiadis. Heaton and Britton had leading roles and a young partnership of importance was initiated in Lynn Seymour and Donald MacLeary.

Lynn Seymour and Donald MacLeary as the Two Adolescents, in 'The Burrow'.

(Above, left) Margot Fonteyn and Michael Somes in 'Ondine'. (Above, right) John Cranko with Antoinette Sibley and Graham Usher in rehearsal. (Below) Robert Helpmann as the Rake and Ray Powell as the Gentleman with a Rope, in 'The Rake's Progress', 1958.

The Royal Charter appeared to have some effect in producing a more stimulating scene. Although MacMillan's *Agon* (August 1958) for Anya Linden had a short life, Ashton returned to form partly, at least, in his next full-length ballet, *Ondine* (October). It was manifestly a vehicle for Fonteyn, and Fonteyn had been an inspiration for him from the days of *Le Baiser de la Fée*. Her entire role as the magical sea spirit was a delight, particularly in the playful Shadow Dance. The score was by Hans Werner Henze and the splendidly histrionic designs by Lila de Nobili.

The enlarged Touring Company was able to stage bigger productions, and in June 1958 added *Le Lac des Cygnes* in its entirety. The leading roles were first danced by Rowena Jackson and Philip Chatfield, and the ballet was given in an important Australasian tour that began in November 1958.

In Australia Helpmann was guest artist, dancing in his own country for the first time. He had returned to Covent Garden the previous May, appearing in some of his finest roles with undiminished effect. In Australia, too, Seymour and MacLeary danced a highly promising *Lac*. The Touring Company was an excellent training ground and many débuts are recorded, among them Antoinette Sibley's first Aurora, in South Africa in 1960.

(Right) The last night of the Touring Company's season in Sydney, 1958. The group includes David Blair, Anya Linden, John Field, Robert Helpmann (at rear), John Lanchbery, Rowena Jackson and Philip Chatfield. (Above) The Touring Company's revival of 'The Sleeping Beauty', with Susan Alexander as Princess Aurora.

Ashton's *La Fille Mal Gardée* might well emerge from any general vote as the best loved new ballet of our time. It is almost unique in being a full-length ballet free from weaknesses or padding. It is from start to finish immensely inventive, strong in narrative and characterisation. Its leading roles have produced countless excellent performances, and it seems always to retain its freshness.

Much is owed to the lively score created by John Lanchbery from Ferdinand Hérold's music, and to the entirely appropriate costumes and sets by Osbert Lancaster. It was a charmer from its première on 28 January 1960 when Nerina (Lise), Blair (Colas), Holden (Widow Simone) and Grant (Alain) inaugurated it at Covent Garden. The first cast-change brought forward a deliciously spirited Lise in the young Merle Park.

The association of the two Companies with opera has continued over the years. In the early days the Vic-Wells Ballet supplied the opera company with dancers and choreography where necessary. This lapsed during World War II but afterwards dancers from Sadler's Wells Ballet appeared in operas at Covent Garden, and Sadler's Wells Theatre Ballet danced in operas at Sadler's Wells.

When the two Companies merged in 1956 their involvement in operas at Sadler's Wells ceased. At Covent Garden, Harold Turner was in charge of ballets performed in opera. By the late fifties a separate opera-ballet group existed and for a time this became in essence a period of apprenticeship for dancers between leaving the Royal Ballet School and joining one of the Companies: among them were Lynn Seymour, Vyvyan Lorrayne, Anthony Dowell, Christopher Gable and Gary Sherwood.

Among leading dancers of the Covent Garden Company who have appeared in opera productions at the Royal Opera House are Svetlana Beriosova, in the Kathleen Ferrier *Orpheus* (1953) and Merle Park and Wayne Eagling in *Die Fledermaus* (1979).

'La Fille Mal Gardée'. (Opposite, above) Merle Park as Lise ; (below) Nadia Nerina as Lise, David Blair as Colas. (Inset) Stanley Holden as Widow Simone, Leslie Edwards as Thomas and Alexander Grant as Alain.
(Below) The Opera Ballet in 'Orpheus and Eurydice'.

Having staged a winner for the Covent Garden Company in *La Fille Mal Gardée*, Ashton produced a popular work, if a less perfect one, for the Touring Company in *The Two Pigeons* (February 1961). He was choreographing for some very rewarding talent in Seymour, Gable and Elizabeth Anderton. They were ideal for the roles: Seymour uniting gamine and lyrical qualities as the Girl, Gable an impetuous and ardent Young Man, and Anderton a dynamic and provocative Gypsy. There was a gently romantic score by Messager and extremely pretty designs by Jacques Dupont.

Seymour's range had been made evident by her sensational creation in November 1960 of the Girl in MacMillan's *The Invitation*. This was the first Company ballet to have an explicit scene of rape, and the whole theme of betrayed innocence, like the neurotic mood of *The Burrow*, heralded a MacMillan preoccupation with corruption that was to dominate the sixties and seventies. The ballet was effective, and Seymour was one of an outstanding group of principals, with Heaton and Doyle as the wife and husband, and Gable as her boy cousin. The score was commissioned from Matyas Seiber and the designs were by Georgiadis.

'The Invitation'. (Left) Lynn Seymour as the Girl and Desmond Doyle as the Husband, in the rape scene. (Inset) Anne Heaton as the Wife, Christopher Gable as the Cousin. (Right) 'The Two Pigeons'. Gable as the Young Man, with (above) Lynn Seymour as the Young Girl and (below) Elizabeth Anderton as a Gypsy Girl.

1961

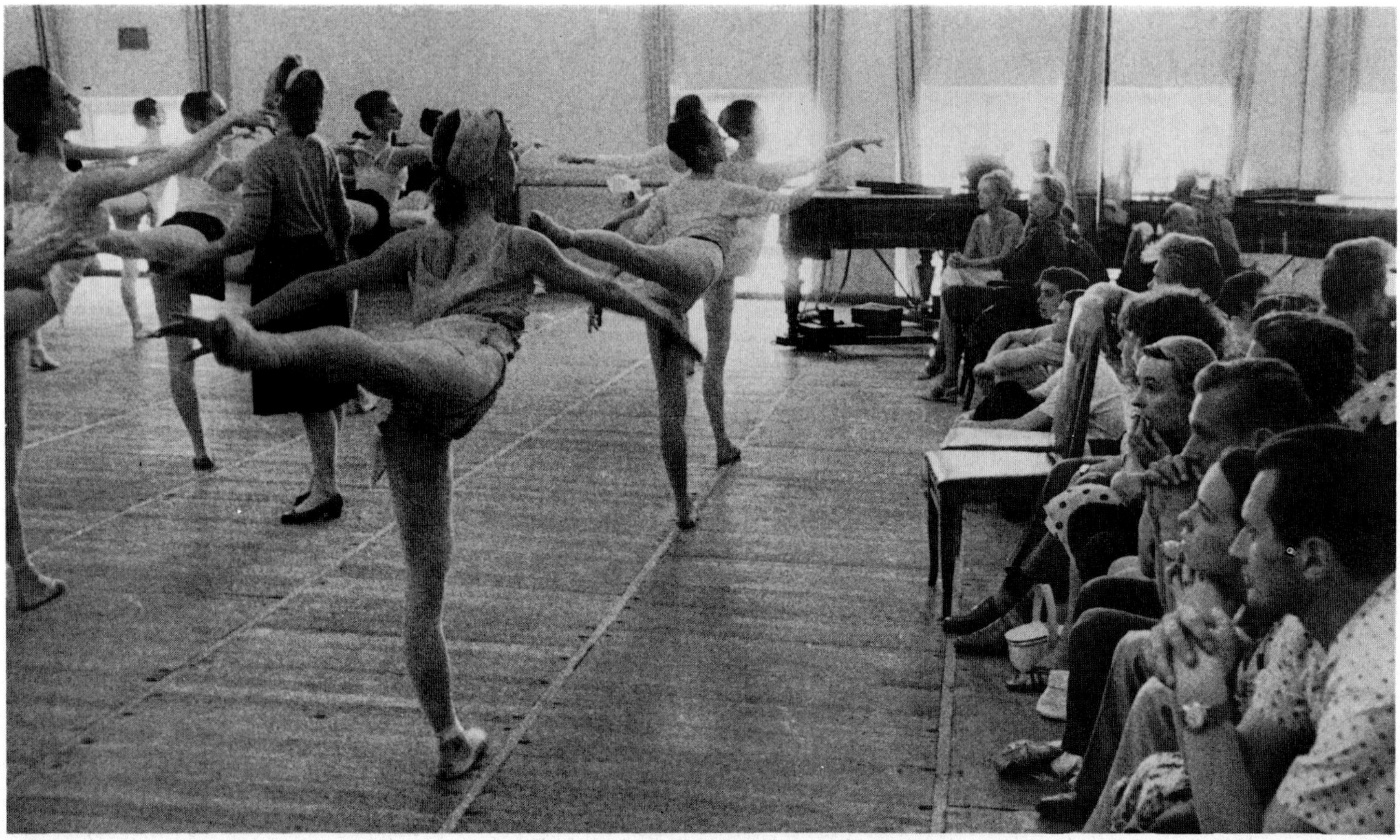

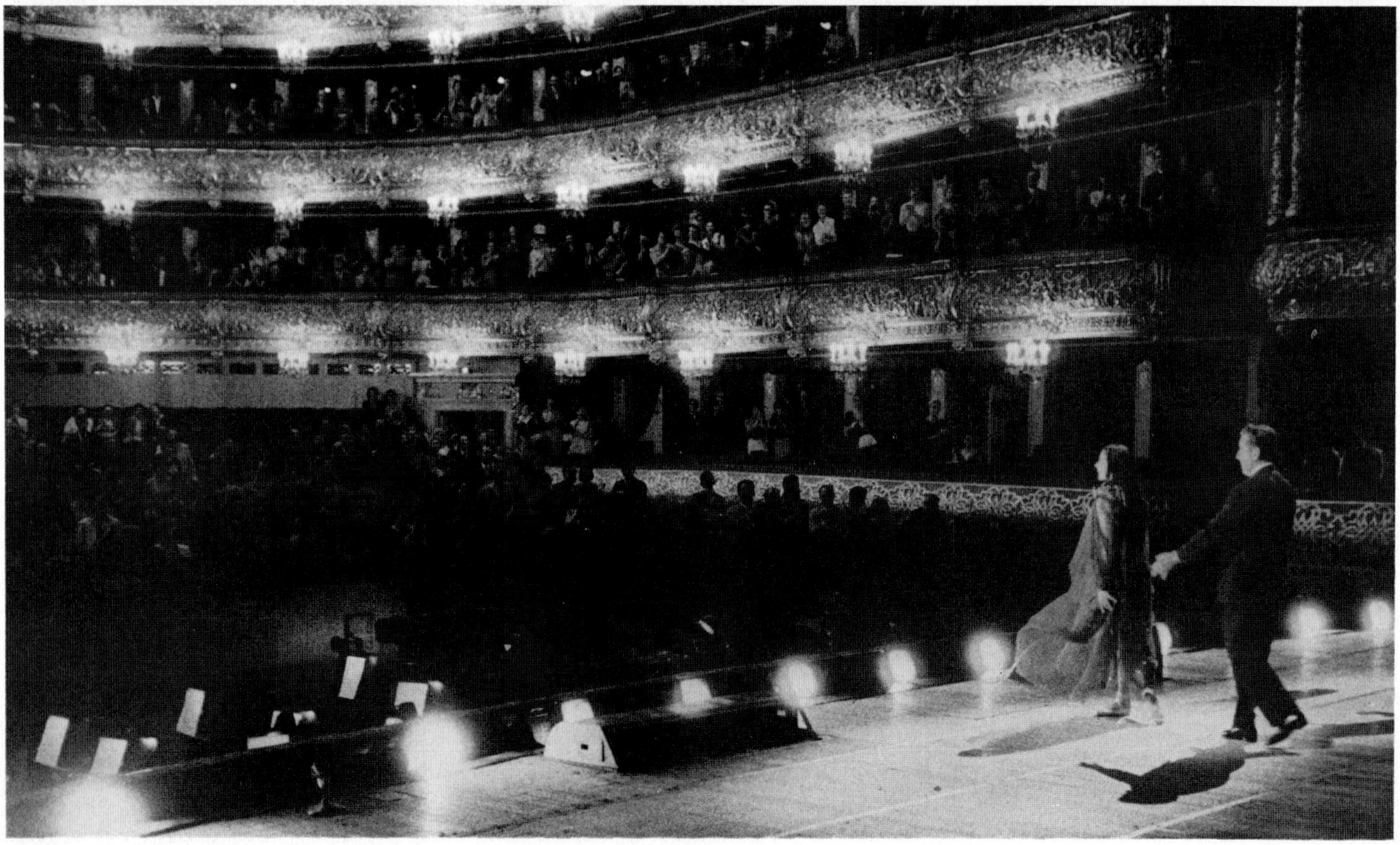

放送を通してみた
東西音楽祭

NHK 27

東京世界音楽祭と大阪国際フェスティバルが、ともに六日で幕を閉じた。わが国の音楽界はじまっていらいの外来演奏家ラッシュを招いたほどの祭典だっただけに、ラジオ・テレビにも外来演奏家の

テレビ中継されたロイヤル・バレエの「ダンス・コンセルタント」

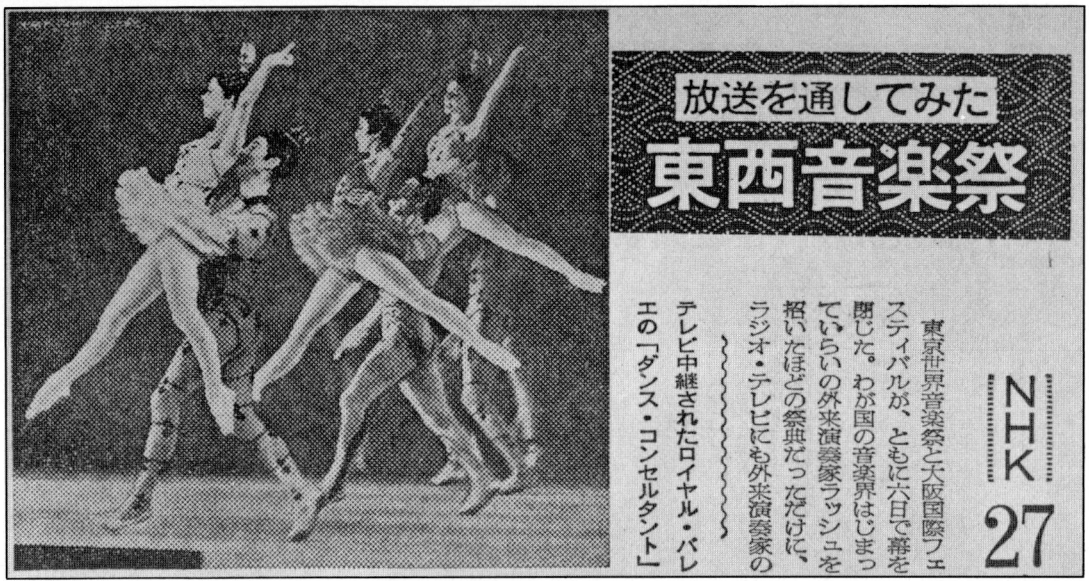

Overseas touring was on the Covent Garden Company's schedule as well as the Touring Company's, and probably the most challenging and prestigious of all their distant dates was their visit to Leningrad and Moscow in June and July 1961. The repertoire for the visit was *Ondine* for the opening night; *The Sleeping Beauty* with Fonteyn and Somes; *La Fille Mal Gardée* with Nerina and Blair; and some short ballets including *The Rake's Progress* and *The Lady and the Fool*. The importance of the engagement lay perhaps in the rapprochement between British and Russian artists and the opportunities for each side to watch and appreciate the technical achievements of the other.

Meanwhile the Touring Company went even farther afield. In April 1961 they were in Tokyo and Osaka, Hong Kong and Manila, and in August and September they appeared at the Baalbek Festival, in Damascus, and in Athens at the beautiful Herodes Atticus Theatre.

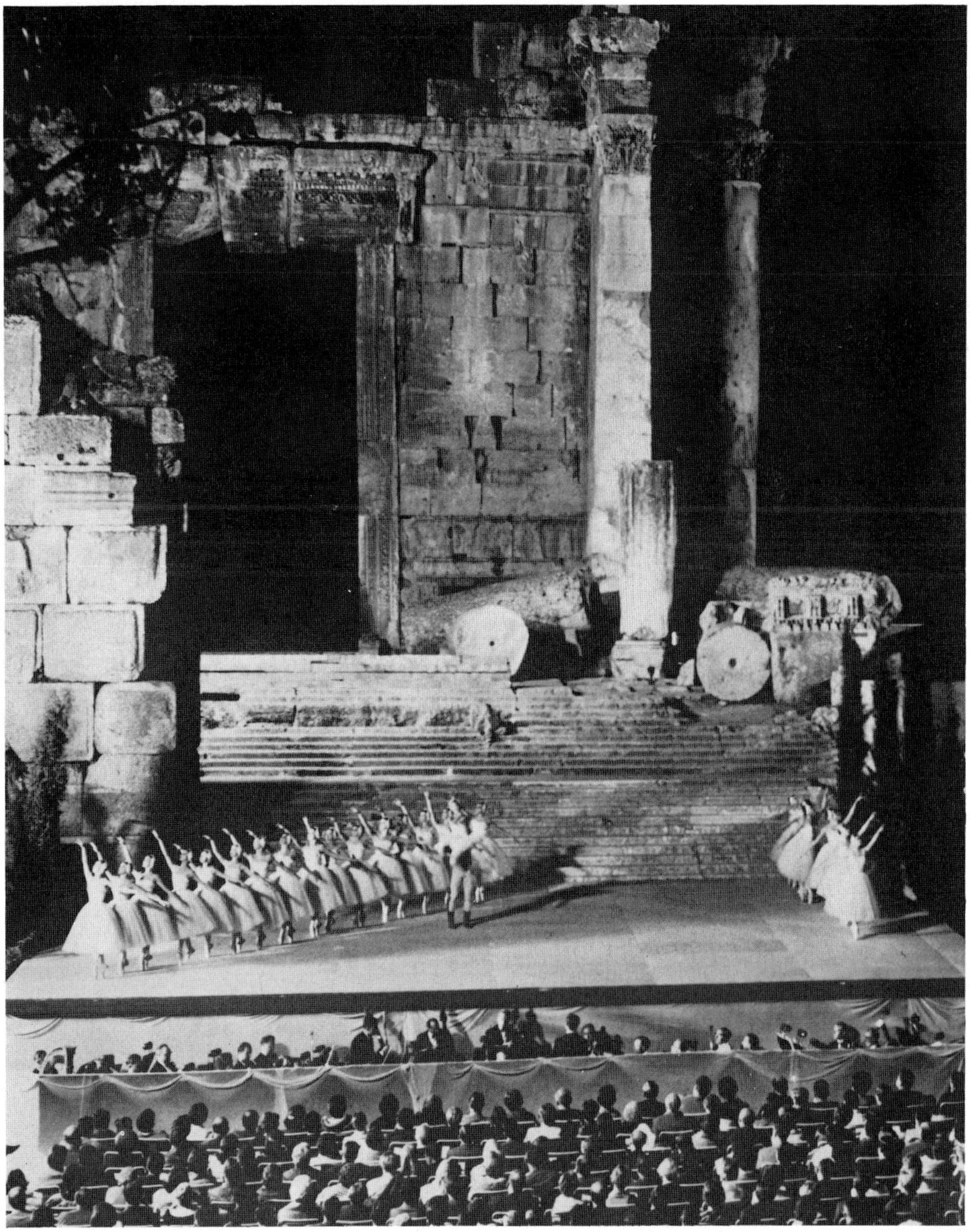

(Left, above) Members of the Bolshoi Ballet watching the Royal Ballet at class during their visit to Moscow; (below) Margot Fonteyn and Frederick Ashton acknowledging the ovation after the opening performance of 'Ondine' at the Kirov Theatre, Leningrad. (Right, above) Notice in a Japanese newspaper during the Touring Company's visit. (Right) The Touring Company in 'Swan Lake' at Baalbek.

1962

The Touring Company was finding a new image under John Field. They were doing it the hard way, in constant provincial journeys that earned them the affection and admiration of the important audiences outside London and gave them a splendid team identity. They played recurring dates in Scotland and Wales, in Eire and Northern Ireland, and through England from South to North. Although dancers 'sent out' from Covent Garden, such as Nerina and Beriosova, Linden and Page, made appearances with them – as occasionally did foreign guest artists such as Melissa Hayden and Flemming Flindt – they were producing their own principals.

Dancers of the sixties on tour have been almost forgotten in recent years. The first of the Touring Company's own Auroras, for instance, when they staged *The Sleeping Beauty* (1959), was Susan Alexander; and Elizabeth Anderton and Judith Maden both danced Aurora in the early sixties. Ian Hamilton and Richard Farley were mainstays of the Company, and Alexander Bennett, who had been principal dancer with the old classical Ballet Rambert, joined the Royal in 1963. Shirley Grahame danced Odette-Odile regularly. When *Fille* was taken into the repertoire in November 1962, it was danced first by Nerina and Sibley and was then entrusted to Doreen Wells. The second night of this production launched Ronald Emblen as Widow Simone, a superbly comic performance that has rightly become a classic of its time. The triple bills toured by the Sadlers Wells Company included *Checkmate, Hamlet, The Invitation, Solitaire* and *Les Patineurs*, and they had their original ballets – sharing at this time the other Company's bad luck with new productions.

(Left) On Tour: Sheila Humphreys waiting for a train. (Below) On Tour: 'Swan Lake', with Shirley Grahame as Odette, Alexander Bennett as Prince Siegfried. (Opposite page) Ronald Emblen as Widow Simone in the Touring Company production of 'La Fille Mal Gardée'.

1962–1963

(Above) Monica Mason as the Chosen Maiden in 'The Rite of Spring'. (Right) Margot Fonteyn and Rudolf Nureyev in 'Marguerite and Armand'. (Inset) Nureyev in 'Le Corsaire'.

The era of the Soviet defectors and their potent influence was at hand. Twenty-four-year-old Rudolf Nureyev, the talking point of London ballet conversation after his appearance at Fonteyn's Gala for the Royal Academy of Dancing in February 1962, in November swept onto the Covent Garden stage in *Le Corsaire*. The partnership with Fonteyn that carried both of them to heights of international fame had begun. Nureyev also provided for The Royal Ballet a much needed stimulus, and their young male dancers, especially Anthony Dowell, were to respond to the pressure.

In *Marguerite and Armand* (March 1963) Ashton (who had been knighted in 1962), composed for Fonteyn and Nureyev a passionate and romantic ballet based on *La Dame aux Camélias*. Echoes of the *Apparitions* ballroom scene were invoked by Beaton's costumes, and the youthful Nureyev flung himself fervently into his first great chance in the Western world. The year before, MacMillan had taken a considerable step forward with a finely concerted choreography for Stravinsky's *The Rite of Spring* (May 1962). Magnificently designed by Sidney Nolan with Australian aboriginal overtones, it set the corps de ballet dancing with a great sense of purpose and revealed Monica Mason's remarkable strength and stamina and her ability to commit herself to an emotional role.

1963

(Above) The corps de ballet in the Kingdom of the Shades scene, Act IV of 'La Bayadère'. (Right) The corps de ballet in Frederick Ashton's Act IV of 'Swan Lake'.

It was not only in *The Rite of Spring* that the Covent Garden corps de ballet were beginning to be the admired of all admirers. Under Ballet Mistress Jill Gregory, who had been with the Vic-Wells Ballet in the early days and returned during the war, the girls were taking pride in their discipline in the great classical ensembles. Flocks of swans had never been more enchanting in their corporate poetry and they were seen to particular advantage in a new Act IV choreographed by Ashton (December 1963) when he and Helpmann collaborated on an imaginative but briefly surviving production of the ballet which is now called *Swan Lake*.

The corps de ballet were given their supreme test and accolade in Nureyev's staging of the Kingdom of Shades scene from *La Bayadère* (November 1963). This had been seen in London when the Kirov danced it in July 1961, and was now welcomed by a public who appreciated its technical intricacies and classical purity. The leading roles were danced by Fonteyn and Nureyev and the first three soloists in the great variations were Park, Mason and Seymour.

1963–1964

(Left) Antoinette Sibley as Titania and Anthony Dowell as Oberon in 'The Dream'. (Below, left) Bronislava Nijinska with Frederick Ashton, David Blair, and Georgina Parkinson at a rehearsal of 'Les Biches'. (Below, right) Annette Page, David Blair and Svetlana Beriosova in 'Serenade'. (Right) Both companies assembled to honour Dame Ninette de Valois on her retirement as Director.

With characteristic decisiveness, de Valois handed over the artistic direction of The Royal Ballet in 1963 when she was sixty-five. Her heir was Ashton, supported by three assistant directors: Somes, Hart and, for the Touring Company, Field. Ashton's first season, from September 1963, began with La Bayadère and the revised Swan Lake.

Shakespeare's quatercentenary arrived in April 1964 and a special programme was staged: Helpmann's Hamlet and new ballets from MacMillan (Images of Love) and Ashton (The Dream). The Dream was instantly loved for its sparkling choreography and sense of fun, and was notable in its launching of a superb partnership of young

dancers, Antoinette Sibley and Anthony Dowell, as Titania and Oberon. Both had been developed in the Royal Ballet School. Sibley had earned headlines in 1960, at 21, by dancing Odette-Odile at short notice when Nerina was indisposed. Dowell had caught attention in the Napoli divertissement staged in May 1962. Now, Ashton's unerring instinct for revealing the individual qualities of dancers gave Sibley and Dowell their stepping stone to fame.

Due to Ashton's admiration for Nijinska, dating from his time with the Ida Rubinstein company, two of her greatest ballets were now acquired for Covent Garden. She arrived in 1962 to rehearse the first of these, Les Biches, and working

with her was a major experience for the dancers. The ballet sounded and looked delightful, with its Poulenc score and Marie Laurencin designs. Honours of performance went to Beriosova, Nijinska's choice for her own role of The Hostess, and the beautiful Georgina Parkinson, who captured the androgynous mystery of the Garçonne.

As a formal, if partial, farewell to de Valois, who was still Principal of the Royal Ballet School, the Company arranged a traditional Defilé on 6 May 1964. This balletic equivalent of a march-past was an imposing exhibition of how the original six dancers had miraculously multiplied into two companies and a large professional school.

Prokofiev's *Romeo and Juliet* had been first seen in London in the superb performance of Galina Ulanova with the Bolshoi Ballet in 1956. It was an obvious possibility for a British choreographer, and now Kenneth MacMillan undertook it for The Royal Ballet. His frequent design collaborator, Nicholas Georgiadis, gave it an air of opulent splendour, and MacMillan proved, in his treatment of the central characters, his increasing mastery of the exquisite art of choreographic duet. The leading roles first danced to great acclaim by Fonteyn and Nureyev have revealed different aspects with succeeding, equally outstanding, performances. MacMillan's special ballerina,

Seymour, with Gable, shared the initial period. Later partnerships included the supremely musical interpretation of Sibley and Dowell, the romantic emphasis of Park, moving from her early status of sparkling soubrette into dramatic ballet, with Donald MacLeary, now an experienced danseur noble.

A long list of entrancing Juliets can be compiled, among them Parkinson, Page, Doreen Wells and Ann Jenner, as well as the fine guest artists Natalia Makarova and Gelsey Kirkland. Character roles were dominantly handled by Somes (Lord Capulet), Farron (Lady Capulet) and Larsen (the Nurse) while Blair created brilliantly the virtuoso mischief of Mercutio.

'Romeo and Juliet'. (Opposite, above) The Ballroom Scene, with Margot Fonteyn as Juliet, Rudolf Nureyev as Romeo, David Blair as Mercutio, and Anthony Dowell as Benvolio; (below) Lynn Seymour and Christopher Gable.
(Above, left) Merle Park and Donald MacLeary. (Above, right) Gerd Larsen as the Nurse, Michael Somes as Capulet, Derek Rencher as Paris. (Left) Antoinette Sibley and Anthony Dowell.

(Overleaf) The redesigned 1965 production of 'Cinderella'. The Ugly Sisters (Frederick Ashton and Robert Helpmann) prepare for the ball. (Inset) The moment when the Sisters, Cinderella (Margot Fonteyn), and their father (Derek Rencher), hear the Fairy Godmother theme.

1965

The Touring Company mounted a new production of *Swan Lake* in May 1965 and took *Raymonda Act III* into their repertoire in May 1966. In fact, the entire *Raymonda* had been staged for them at the Spoleto Festival in July 1964 by Nureyev. It was intended that he should star with Fonteyn, but she had to withdraw, and the title role was danced, delightfully, by Doreen Wells. As a whole the ballet proved boring, but the last divertissement found a place in both repertoires.

Wells and the nineteen-year-old David Wall were fast becoming the accepted principals of the Touring Company. They made an excellent partnership – Wells' delicate and joyous femininity complementing Wall's attractively virile vigour. All round the provinces audiences began to look for the Wells-Wall combination on their programmes and to book accordingly, enjoying them in the classics, in *Fille* and in *The Two Pigeons*.

(Left) Doreen Wells as Odette,
David Wall as Prince Siegfried, in
'Swan Lake'.
(Above) Doreen Wells as Raymonda
and David Wall as Jean de Brienne
in 'Raymonda', Act III.

(Right) 'Les Noces', with Svetlana
Beriosova (centre, top) as the Bride,
Gerd Larsen (at left) and Ray
Roberts, as her Parents. (Below)
Anthony Dowell, Vyvyan Lorrayne
and Robert Mead in 'Monotones 2'.
(Opposite page) 'Song of the Earth'.
Anthony Dowell as the Messenger of
the Death, with (above) Jennifer
Penney and (below) Monica Mason.

The Ashton régime was coinciding with a good spell for the Covent Garden Company. *Les Noces,* an undoubted masterpiece, entered the repertoire in March 1966 with a touching interpretation of the Bride and Groom by Beriosova and Robert Mead, and an effective ensemble led by Parkinson and Dowell.

Ashton had produced a choregraphic gem in March 1965, *Monotones II* to Satie's 'Trois Gymnopédies', a trio of exquisitely balanced bodies in which the creators, Vyvyan Lorrayne, Dowell and Mead remain unequalled. It acquired a companion piece, *Monotones I* (April 1966) to the 'Trois Gnossiennes' and 'Prélude d'Eginhard', danced by Sibley, Parkinson and Shaw.

MacMillan had choreographed Mahler's *Song of the Earth* for the Stuttgart Ballet and now it was restaged for The Royal Ballet (May 1966). One of his most sensitive and distilled creations, it was given a remarkable performance by Mason, MacLeary, and Dowell (Marcia Haydée from the original cast danced on the first night). In the delicately choreographed Third Song, *About Youth,* Jennifer Penney was the essence of carefree innocence.

MacMillan himself had accepted the artistic directorship of the Deutsche Oper in West Berlin, where he remained for three years.

Dowell's steady development was marked by the chance to create the leading role in a ballet by Antony Tudor. Tudor, who had danced with the Vic-Wells Ballet briefly in the thirties and then concentrated on choreography with his own London Ballet and later with Ballet Theatre in America, staged *Shadowplay* (January 1967) to a score by Koechlin with designs by Michael Annals. Dowell's role of the Boy with Matted Hair had 'Jungle Book' connotations and Buddhist implications. Tudor's *Lilac Garden* was revived at Covent Garden with little success (November 1968) and a complex work for the Touring Company, *Knight Errant,* in the same month never established itself.

Nureyev, an international star rover, was still occasionally associated with The Royal Ballet and in February 1968 he choreographed a new production of *The Nutcracker,* the one classic that had never been presented at Covent Garden. Nureyev's version was elaborate and enjoyable, full of new thinking, and building up the leading roles so that the ballerina danced the young heroine as well as the classical duets, and Drosselmeyer became the Nutcracker Prince. Nureyev and Park were the first, and brilliant, protagonists.

The Touring Company acquired one of MacMillan's best pure-dance ballets, the Shostakovitch *Concerto* (May 1967), first staged two months previously in Berlin. The lyrical duet in the second movement, danced by Wells and Richard Farley, has been a test and a triumph for a number of partnerships.

A new Royal Ballet venture, Peter Brinson's 'Ballet for All', planned to take introductory programmes to schools and colleges, began operations in 1964. One of its most ingenious offerings was a comparison between past and present in *Two Coppélias* (1967 expanded 1970) that included a delightful reconstruction of the Paris original by Paulette Dynalix, with Janet Francis as Swanilda and Margaret Barbieri as a travesty Franz.

(Above, left) Doreen Wells and Richard Farley in rehearsal for the second movement of 'Concerto'. (Above) Rudolf Nureyev as Drosselmeyer and Merle Park as Clara in 'The Nutcracker'. (Left) Anthony Dowell as the Boy with Matted Hair and Merle Park as the Celestial in 'Shadowplay'. (Right) Janet Francis as Swanilda, Spencer Parker as the Peasant Boy and Margaret Barbieri as Franz in Ballet for All's 'Two Coppélias'.

1968

Giselle, the oldest ballet in the repertoire, dating from 1841, was given new life by the Touring Company in May 1968 in a staging by Peter Wright, who had danced with Sadler's Wells Theatre Ballet after experience with the Metropolitan Ballet and Ballets Jooss. He had also been Ballet Master and Assistant Director to Cranko in Stuttgart. There he produced a version of Giselle that ranks as one of the best modern revisions and is still danced by Sadler's Wells Royal Ballet. The first Touring Company principals were Wells and Wall, with Shirley Grahame as Myrtha.

New dancers were being featured throughout the Touring Company repertoire. Lucette Aldous, from the classical Ballet Rambert, joined in 1966, steadily augmenting her reputation as a fine prima ballerina. Jane Landon and Piers Beaumont were partners in the traditional ballets. Anderton, the tempestuous Gypsy Girl of The Two Pigeons, proved to be one of the most essentially Romantic Era Giselles, and the young Margaret Barbieri and Nicholas Johnson were an attractive later casting as Giselle and Albrecht. Brenda Last, a fresh and exuberant virtuoso recruited from Western Theatre Ballet, danced Swanilda in 1966 and eventually became one of the most popular of the Company's principals. Paul Clarke, who was to die at a tragically early age, was attracting attention with his good looks and lyrically fluent dancing.

(Above) Doreen Wells as Giselle and David Wall as Albrecht in the crowning of Giselle as Queen of the Vintage. (Right) Brenda Last and Paul Clarke in the peasant pas de six. (Opposite) Margaret Barbieri as Giselle, Nicholas Johnson as Albrecht, Marion Tait as Myrtha, in the Ballet for All series on Thames TV. (Inset) The death of Giselle, with Elizabeth Anderton.

1968

A new production of *The Sleeping Beauty* was planned for Covent Garden and in December 1968 the curtain rose on a totally fresh conception. Staged by Ashton and Peter Wright, with scenery by Henry Bardon and costumes by Lila de Nobili and Rostislav Dobuzhinsky, it had the merit of complete dissimilarity from the Sergeyev-Messel production that had lasted from 1946.

It was not popular but it had great homogeneity. Its Victorian Gothic detail and style, impressive in itself, tended to soften the edge of the glittering Petipa dances and to dominate the choreography, where the earlier designs had emphasised its splendour.

Sibley danced the first gala night with MacLeary; the second night reinforced everyone's belief that Sibley and Dowell made a God-given partnership. The line-up of Fairies (with new titles) included important current talents. Tall and lovely Deanne Bergsma was the Lilac Fairy, and other Fairies on the first night were Ria Peri, Christine Beckley, Jennifer Penney, Parkinson (in a new and bubbling Ashton solo for a Fairy of Joy), Jenner and Mason. Later performances brought in three delightful dancers in Diana Vere, Lesley Collier and Laura Connor. For the first time in the Company's history a woman, Julia Farron, played Carabosse.

(Below, left) Prologue of 'The Sleeping Beauty' with Deanne Bergsma as the Lilac Fairy; on right, Lesley Collier and Ann Jenner. (Left) Antoinette Sibley as Princess Aurora and Anthony Dowell as Prince Florimund. (Below) Act I, the Waltz.

1968

In the early fifties a student of stage design at the Royal College of Art, Julia Trevelyan Oman, sketched out a project for a ballet based on Elgar's *Enigma Variations,* and she showed it to Ashton. In 1966 he began working on the project and in October 1968 it was premièred at Covent Garden.

The accurate and intricate period designs might well have submerged the choreography but in fact they supplied the basis for a series of remarkable dances that united to form a perfect whole. It was probably the most English ballet Britain's national Company had ever produced, celebrating the English genius of the great Victorian era. The tone was set by the inspired interpretation of Derek Rencher and Beriosova as Elgar and his wife, and the mood was sustained throughout by the whole of the original cast. Sibley as Dorabella, Dowell in a fireworks solo as Troyte, were no more apt than Lorrayne and Mead in a romantic duet as Isabel Fitton and Richard Arnold or Doyle's dignity and restraint in the mime role of Jaeger.

(Opposite page) Robert Mead as Richard Arnold, Vyvyan Lorrayne as Isabel Fitton, Desmond Doyle as Jaeger, Anthony Dowell as Troyte, Derek Rencher as Elgar, Svetlana Beriosova as his Wife, Leslie Edwards as Basil Nevinson, Georgina Parkinson as Winifred Norbury, Brian Shaw as Townshend; seated, Antoinette Sibley as Dorabella, Wayne Sleep as Sinclair, Alexander Grant as Baker; at right, Julie Wood and Ronald Plaisted, as Housekeeper and Carrier.
(Left) Antoinette Sibley as Dorabella.
(Below, right) Anthony Dowell as Troyte; (left) Deanne Bergsma as Lady Mary Lygon.

(Right) Rudolf Nureyev as the Traveller in 'The Ropes of Time'.
(Left) Derek Rencher as Minos and Vyvyan Lorrayne as Pasiphaë in Ronald Hynd's 'Pasiphaë', for the Choreographic Group 1969. (Below) David Wall and Alfeda Thorogood, Lucette Aldous and Hendrik Davel in 'In the Beginning'.
(Opposite page) Members of the Company pay tribute to Frederick Ashton. The group around Ashton includes Rudolf Nureyev, Robert Mead, Margot Fonteyn, John Lanchbery, John Hart, Keith Martin, Ann Jenner, Michael Somes, Anthony Twiner, Robert Helpmann, Svetlana Beriosova, Donald Macleary, Antoinette Sibley, Jennifer Penney and Anthony Dowell.

Of the many galas and tributes staged by The Royal Ballet at Covent Garden, probably the most ingenious was the Tribute paid to Ashton when he retired from the artistic directorship. On 24 July, 1970 an audience assembled for a 'mystery tour' – the content of the performance had been kept a complete secret and no printed programme was distributed until after the evening had ended. The whole show, devised and produced by Somes and Hart, followed a nostalgic narrative written by Chappell and entertainingly compèred by Helpmann. Extracts from the Ashton repertoire flowed along in superb sequence, mingling currently familiar work with glimpses from the far past – Bergsma as the

Lady with a Fan from *The Lord of Burleigh* and Grant in Walter Gore's solo from *Rio Grande*.

Before Ashton's retirement a move was made to give professional chances with the Touring Company to two choreographers who had been tried out with Leslie Edwards' Royal Ballet Choreographic Group – Geoffrey Cauley and David Drew. Cauley's *In the Beginning* (January 1969) cast Alfreda Thorogood, David Wall, Lucette Aldous and Hendrik Davel in an attractively original use of the Adam and Eve theme. Drew began with *Intrusion* (January 1969), originally staged for the Choreographic Group with Royal Ballet School students, and he choreographed four more ballets in the next four years. The last

production at Covent Garden under Ashton's directorship was also forward-looking. Rudi van Dantzig's *The Ropes of Time*, (March 1970) for Nureyev, Mason and Diana Vere, used a score by the Dutch composer of electronic music, Jan Boerman. Ashton was succeeded by a joint directorship of MacMillan and Field which ended when Field resigned in December 1970. MacMillan remained as artistic director with Peter Wright as assistant director with special charge of the Touring Company. A total reshuffle occurred, and the Touring Company, severely reduced in numbers, was changed into an experimental New Group. This plan did not work well, however, and was soon abandoned.

'Dances at a Gathering'. (Above) Rudolf Nureyev, Laura Connor and Ann Jenner. (Right) Antoinette Sibley and Anthony Dowell. (Opposite, above) Deanne Bergsma, Desmond Kelly, Nicholas Johnson in 'Field Figures'; (below) 'Apollo'. Desmond Kelly, with Deanne Bergsma as Terpsichore, Vergie Derman as Polyhymnia, Vyvyan Lorrayne as Calliope.

The Royal Ballet now entered on a period when original creations were outnumbered by acquisitions from other companies, usually from America or Holland. Balanchine's *Serenade* and *Apollo* had been staged in 1964 and 1966 respectively by the Covent Garden Company. In 1970 *Apollo* was added to the Touring Company repertoire, danced by Desmond Kelly, who had joined them from the National Ballet of Washington and who was a fine interpreter of traditional princes. His range, however, easily embraced *Apollo* and extended to Glen Tetley's *Field Figures* (November 1970), a modern work to an electronic score by Stockhausen in which Kelly and Bergsma, Vergie Derman and Nicholas Johnson proved how splendidly classically trained dancers can interpret other forms of choreography.

Jerome Robbins was stylistically easier for The Royal Ballet than Balanchine and *Dances at a Gathering* (October 1970), modulated to suit the chosen cast, was a delight. Its relaxed and romantic mood, contrasting lyrical duets with gently humorous sequences, appealed to most people and the dancers were uniformly excellent. Nureyev in the anchor role, Sibley and Dowell in a silky love duet, Mason with the ebullient Michael Coleman, and Seymour (returned with MacMillan from Berlin) in a witty flirtation scene, were the precursors of many attractive permutations of performers.

1971

The popularity of full-length ballets made the creation of new ones imperative and MacMillan decided to expand a fine one-act ballet, *Anastasia*, composed in Berlin to music by Martinu in 1967. He added, in July 1971, two earlier acts to Tchaikovsky symphonies, with designs by Barry Kay. Seymour, who had created the original ballet, backtracked from the girl in the mental home to the teenage Russian Grand Duchess with deep involvement and dramatic power.

The Touring Company, trying to popularise its image, staged a genuinely funny piece, *The Grand Tour* (February 1971) by Joe Layton, set to a selection of Noël Coward songs and assembling idols of the thirties on a cruise liner with a middle-aged American lady. Lorrayne revealed a delightful comic gift as the awkward and endearing tourist, and in a sentimental but charming duet she was partnered by Stephen Jefferies as a Steward.

Jefferies was rapidly building up a reputation. His performance in *The Rake's Progress* in 1970, after only one year with the Company, established him as a dance-actor of great potential.

'Anastasia'. (Above) From left to right, Leslie Edwards as an Aide-de-Camp, Gerd Larsen as Anna Vryubova, Derek Rencher as Tsar Nicholas II, Adrian Grater as Rasputin, Svetlana Beriosova as the Tsarina, Lynn Seymour as Anastasia. (Below) Lynn Seymour in the title role.

(Left) 'The Grand Tour', with, from left to right, Brenda Last and Wayne Sleep as Stowaways, Deirdre O'Conaire as Gertrude Lawrence, Sheila Humphreys as Theda Bara, Paul Clarke as Douglas Fairbanks, Gary Sherwood as Noël Coward, Doreen Wells as Mary Pickford, David Drew as G. B. Shaw; Stephen Jefferies, Donald Kirkpatrick and David Gordon as Stewards; at rear, Nicholas Johnson as Gertrude Stein, Jeanetta Laurence as Alice B. Toklas. (Below) Stephen Jefferies in 'The Rake's Progress'.

The Robbins' connection continued with his cool, evocative duet, *Afternoon of a Faun* (December 1971), memorably danced by Sibley and Dowell. It was a happier choice than his *Requiem Canticles* (November 1972). The Covent Garden Company also tried once more to adapt to a Balanchine programme in January 1973 with *The Four Temperaments, Agon* and *Prodigal Son*. The last, dating from the common ground of the Diaghilev Ballet rather than the specialised style of New York City Ballet, emerged well and strongly, especially when the ballet was taken over later in 1973 by the Touring Company. Of the various dancers of the Prodigal Son, Nureyev, Desmond Kelly and Stephen Jefferies have been deeply impressive. Fonteyn

(Opposite, above) Antoinette Sibley and Anthony Dowell in 'Afternoon of a Faun'; (below) 'Triad', with Dowell as the Boy, Eagling as his Brother, Sibley as the Girl. (Left) Ann Jenner as the Gypsy Girl in 'The Two Pigeons'. (Below) Natalia Makarova in the pas de deux from 'Don Quixote'.

danced (February 1972) in the revival of *Poème de l'Extase,* a ballet created for her in Stuttgart by Cranko. This was more satisfying in design than in dance, with magnificent sets and costumes by Jürgen Rose in the manner of Klimt.

MacMillan followed *Anastasia* with *Triad,* created in January 1972 at Covent Garden by Sibley, Dowell, and a dancer of promising technical ability, Wayne Eagling. In complete contrast MacMillan produced the effectively theatrical *The Seven Deadly Sins* (July 1973) which revealed a new and provocative aspect of Jennifer Penney.

1972 was the year of Natalia Makarova's first guest appearances with the Company in her completely individual and fascinating readings of Giselle and Odette-Odile and in the *Don Quixote* pas de deux.

The Touring Company was acquiring a wide range of short modern works. One that they seemed to slip into easily was Hans van Manen's *Grosse Fuge* (April 1972), for an octet of dancers who originally included the smooth and attractive Patricia Ruanne. Van Manen's inventive and rather casual style worked admirably for this Company, as did his effective duet, *Twilight,* which Ruanne danced with the increasingly effective Paul Clarke. They had staged Herbert Ross's chilling ballet, *The Maids* (October 1971) based on Genet's play, in which the central duo was brilliantly danced by Kerrison Cooke and Nicholas Johnson. MacMillan's *Las Hermanas* (June 1971) was superbly interpreted by Seymour and Gary Sherwood with Barbieri as the haunting youngest sister.

The later ballets staged by Cranko for The Royal Ballet had been surprisingly unsuccessful. *Antigone* (October 1959) for instance had been excellently created by Beriosova and MacLeary but faded fairly rapidly. Cranko had then gone on to the Stuttgart Ballet. In 1966 he staged *Brandenburg Nos. 2 and 4* at Covent Garden and at the same time revived his *Card Game.* Neither had been popular; but in October 1973 *Card Game* was transferred to the Touring Company at Sadler's Wells and given a witty and enjoyable performance by Jefferies, Lorrayne and Barbieri.

(Opposite, top left) Nicholas Johnson as Claire, Kerrison Cooke as Solange in 'The Maids'; (right) Stephen Jefferies as the Joker in 'Card Game'; (below) Carole Hill, Stephen Jefferies, Margaret Barbieri, Kerrison Cooke and Paul Clarke in 'Grosse Fuge'. (Below) Patricia Ruanne and Paul Clarke in 'Twilight'.

MacMillan's *Manon* (March 1974) has gained greatly in coordination and impulsion since its opening night but even then the superb trio of performances by Sibley, Dowell and Wall were greatly appreciated. Later interpreters of the title role have given it varied emphasis but Sibley's account of innocence destroyed was subtlety itself and, as always, she and Dowell related dance to music with immaculate accuracy. Wall stole the honours in the demi-monde soirée by an assured and immensely funny drunken dance and duet with Mason. Rencher produced a masterly creation as the callous Monsieur GM.

A MacMillan work in total contrast emerged in October with *Elite Syncopations,* and the ballet looked even better in the unorthodox setting of the Big Top in Battersea Park the following June. Stridently coloured designs by Ian Spurling matched to ragtime elicited witty performances, especially perhaps from Park and MacLeary and, in a variant of the short-man-tall-girl comedy, Vergie Derman and Wayne Sleep. Sleep, one of the most idiosyncratic and extrovert personalities produced by The Royal Ballet, has had an immediate rapport with audiences from his graduating performance in *Les Patineurs* in 1966.

(Left) Antoinette Sibley as Manon, Anthony Dowell as des Grieux in 'Manon'. (Below) Jennifer Penney as Manon, David Wall as Lescaut.

116

(Above and right) Vergie Derman and Wayne Sleep, Merle Park and Michael Coleman, in 'Elite Syncopations'. (Top) The 25th anniversary of the Company's first visit to New York: members of the Company who were on both tours, from left, Joyce Wells (wardrobe), Alexander Grant, Jill Gregory (Ballet Mistress, kneeling), Kenneth MacMillan, Gerd Larsen, Leslie Edwards, Brian Shaw (kneeling), Michael Somes, Henry Legerton. (Far right) The 'Big Top'.

1975–1976

Robbins again provided one of the delights of the repertoire when the company acquired *The Concert* (March 1975). Its zany humour was exactly right for the Royal Ballet temperament and a succession of lively characterisations have set audiences chuckling. Seymour shared feminine honours with Parkinson (unforgettable as the lady with a blue toque). Coleman and Wall alternately danced the henpecked husband with relish, and Graham Fletcher, a consistently interesting and brilliant dancer in a variety of roles, played the terrified young man to perfection. Anthony Twiner, as the on-stage pianist, combined comedy with a meticulous interpretation of the score.

Seymour earned one of her finest creations in February 1976 when Ashton and Julia Trevelyan Oman again collaborated, this time with *A Month in the Country*. Seymour's delicate footwork and fluttering, conversational hands exquisitely represented the volatile nature of Turgenev's Natalia Petrovna.

Tetley's second ballet for the Company, *Laborintus* (July 1972), extremely modern in content to a score by Berio, had not succeeded in spite of Seymour and Nureyev. Now the main company took over *Voluntaries* (November 1976), the work he had staged for the Stuttgart Ballet as a tribute to Cranko, who had died suddenly in 1973. A work more in the classical tradition, it suited both the dancers and the public. Seymour (and later Alfreda Thorogood) and Wall danced it with passionate intensity.

(Left) Bus-ride in Korea, 1975.
(Left, below) 'The Concert', with
Georgina Parkinson and Michael
Coleman, Lynn Seymour and
Graham Fletcher. (Right) Lynn
Seymour and Anthony Dowell in 'A
Month in the Country'. (Below)
Alfreda Thorogood and David Wall
in 'Voluntaries'.

1976–1977

A trio of Japanese-inspired ballets was introduced in 1975/76. The Covent Garden Company's *Rituals* (MacMillan, December 1975) was sandwiched between *Shukumei* (February 1975) by Jack Carter, a prolific freelance choreographer of great theatrical flair, and Lynn Seymour's *Rashomon* (October 1976), both staged by the Touring Company. All three had strength and character, and were given fine performances. The most memorable was Marion Tait's vengeful widow of *Shukumei* – and Tait's variety was beginning to show in the comedy of *Card Game* and the classical manoeuvres of *Les Rendezvous*.

Summertide (October 1976) was Peter Wright's sixth ballet for the Company which he directs to admirable purpose and which from September 1976 became Sadler's Wells Royal Ballet. Other choreographers – Ronald Hynd, Christopher Bruce, Ashley Killar, David Morse and André Prokovsky – had all staged ballets that helped to stretch and develop the new young dancers of the late seventies.

One work that encouraged budding feminine talent was Lynn Seymour's *The Court of Love* (April 1977) in which Susan Lucas and Susan Fitzgerald were happily cast as the Maiden and the Enchantress.

1978

Mayerling (February 1978) is probably the most talked of and written about ballet in the repertoire. Immensely ambitious, it dealt (as had *Anastasia*) with real people out of recent history and with a controversial subject. It was thoroughly researched by Gillian Freeman for her scenario and turned out to suit, and extend, MacMillan's particular genius for pas de deux. The central character, Crown Prince Rudolf of Austria, was shown almost entirely in duets with various women: mother, wife, first mistress, second mistress, third mistress (Mary Vetsera). The background was filled in through crowd scenes, and lavishly dressed by Georgiadis.

Three casts carried the early performances. Created with force and commitment by Seymour with Wall – it is very much the man's ballet – it was later danced by Collier (a ballerina of immense purity of line and keen intelligence) with Eagling; and by the sensitive and touching Alfreda Thorogood, with Stephen Jefferies at his most spectacular. Other roles were equally well depicted. Wendy Ellis painted a sincere and moving portrait of the terrified Princess Stephanie; Park was a brilliantly worldly Countess Larisch; and Parkinson gave grace and dignity to the Empress Elisabeth. Sandra Conley, in a later casting, set this role even more keenly in context.

'Mayerling'. (Opposite, above)
David Wall as Crown Prince Rudolf,
Lynn Seymour as Mary Vetsera;
(below) Wayne Eagling and Lesley
Collier; (left) Stephen Jefferies and
Alfreda Thorogood. (Below, left)
Gerd Larsen as Baroness Vetsera,
Merle Park as Countess Larisch.
(Right) Wendy Ellis as Princess
Stephanie.

1978–1979

Celebrations again produced a birthday performance at Sadler's Wells for de Valois, who was eighty on 6 June 1978, and a 60th Birthday Tribute to Fonteyn at Covent Garden on 23 May 1979. Fonteyn appeared, surrounded by flowers and briefly accompanied by Ashton, in a solo, *Salut d'Amour à Margot Fonteyn*, which he had woven out of memories of all her greatest roles. She then danced the Tango in *Façade* with Helpmann. Forty years on – and the three young artists of the thirties were now secure in international fame. Fonteyn had been created a Dame of the British Empire in 1956 and Helpmann was knighted in 1968.

The de Valois evening (26 September 1978) brought birthday ballets from MacMillan (6.6.78) and the latest new choreographer, David Bintley (*Take Five*). Bintley, a product of the Choreographic Group, had staged *The Outsider* (March 1978) for the Sadler's Wells Royal Ballet – a firm, melodramatic ballet with good roles for Lois Strike, Stephen Wicks and David Morse.

Drama suited the Sadler's Wells Royal Ballet. They had tackled with dedication MacMillan's grim *Playground* (August 1979) about a group of mental patients and their fantasy world. Especially admirable were Tait as the awkward, immature central character and Siobhan Stanley as the self-elected mother figure.

(Opposite, above) David Morse as Dariol, Lois Strike as Renée, Stephen Wicks (at window) as Meursault in 'The Outsider'; (below) Desmond Kelly as a Youth, Marion Tait as the Girl with Make-up, Siobhan Stanley as her Mother, in 'Playground'. (Left) Dame Ninette de Valois at Sadler's Wells for the performance on 26 September 1978 to celebrate her 80th birthday; on her right is Alicia Markova. (Below) Dame Margot Fonteyn celebrating her 60th birthday at the Royal Opera House, with Sir Robert Helpmann in the tango from 'Façade'.

1980

(Above, left) Margaret Barbieri as Papillon and Stephen Jefferies as the Shah in 'Papillon'. (Below) Barbieri and Derek Purnell as Light Moon, June Highwood and Stephen Wicks as Dark Moon, in 'Day into Night'.

(Above) Galina Samsova and David Ashmole in 'Paquita' with, from left, June Highwood, Sherilyn Kennedy, Janis Parsons, Samira Saidi, Claire Farnsworth, Nicola Katrak, Bess Dales, Susan Lucas, Susan Crow, Franziska Merky, Jennifer Mills.

Galina Samsova, for many years prima ballerina of London Festival Ballet, reached The Royal Ballet by way of a small classical company run with her husband André Prokovsky. Trained in Kiev, Samsova enhanced every role she undertook by her technical purity and unforced ability to display classical 'adage'. Originally a guest artist, she became principal dancer and teacher to Sadler's Wells Royal Ballet in 1980 and staged *Paquita* for them in April. Her influence and example sharpened presentation and technique in soloists and corps de ballet alike. In *Paquita* she danced with David Ashmole, who had transferred from Covent Garden in 1976 and was sharing the leading male roles with Alain Dubreuil, Desmond Kelly and Carl Myers.

Ronald Hynd's *Papillon* (February 1980) was taken over from the Houston Ballet. A send-up of Romantic Ballet, full of deliberate quotes from familiar works and set to an attractive Offenbach score, it outraged purists but proved to be popular with the general ballet-going public. Another Choreographic Group discovery, Michael Corder, demonstrated a pleasing and promising talent for using his chosen dancers in *Day into Night* (March 1980).

1980

Long before it was The Royal Ballet, the Company had received warm Royal patronage, especially from HM Queen Elizabeth The Queen Mother and HRH The Princess Margaret. On the evening of The Queen Mother's 80th birthday (4 August 1980) she and her family attended a gala at Covent Garden for which Ashton staged a glitteringly virtuoso ballet, *Rhapsody*. Set to Rachmaninov's 'Rhapsody on a Theme of Paganini', it was created for Mikhail Baryshnikov, who had first danced as guest artist with the Company in 1975, and it included a role for Collier that exploited her marvellously delicate speed and secure balances. It was a scintillating birthday gift, in the best tradition of court entertainment.

In *Gloria* (March 1980) at Covent Garden MacMillan had matched a remarkable ease of creative invention to a deep and powerful response to music. Poulenc's 'Gloria in G Major' was opposed in content to the theme of mourning for the lost generation of World War I, but the pose and movement of the dance excitingly matched the score's dynamics. The first leading trio, Penney, Eagling and Julian Hosking, interpreted the physical patterns meticulously.

The Sleeping Beauty, with its many solo roles, always stresses potential, and the Fairy and Cavalier line-up in 1980 included new soloists who were being tipped as future winners. A year later even newer names were being heard – Fiona Chadwick, Bryony Brind and Philip Broomhead.

(Left, above) Jennifer Penney, Julian Hosking and Wayne Eagling in 'Gloria'; (below) Lesley Collier as Odette, David Wall as Prince Siegfried, in Norman Morrice's 1979 production of 'Swan Lake'. (Right) Collier with Mikhail Baryshnikov in 'Rhapsody'. (Below) 'The Sleeping Beauty': Fairies with their Cavaliers, from left Julie Rose and Nicolas Dixon, Genesia Rosato and Antony Dowson, Pippa Wylde and Derek Deane, Deirdre Eyden and Ashley Page, Angela Cox and Matthew Hawkins, Jennifer Jackson and Ross MacGibbon.

From the beginning the Company was supported by a school. In 1947 this became a fully educational institution based in Talgarth Road, Barons Court, London and by 1951 it was recognised by the Ministry of Education. White Lodge, Richmond, the present elegant setting for the Junior School, was acquired in 1955 and the Upper School premises at Talgarth Road were expanded.

The importance of a school to a major ballet company is self-evident and the importance of the Royal Ballet School to Great Britain has been proved time and time again by graduates (such as Sibley and Dowell) who have become well-loved principals with the Company. The organisation is now considerable, with a large staff and a well devised and wide curriculum.

Annual Royal Ballet School performances, initiated in 1959, have become a tradition. They are vital to the development of dancers who need to get the feel of a theatre, and they are of enormous interest to the balletgoer, who can trace the progress of pupils through the years.

The Two Pigeons has been an especially fruitful School performance ballet. In 1965 it was danced by Collier, Barbieri, Graham Powell and Nicholas Johnson, and in 1975 by Nicola Katrak, Chenca Williams, Stephen Beagley and Ashley Page. One exciting matinée introduced Mark Silver as Oberon in *The Dream* (1973).

A popular item of School performances has been the Morris and Folk Dances, and the boys' Morris team, for which Jonathan Burrows at one point proved a particularly efficient and engaging Foreman, has also appeared in Folk Dance Festivals.

(Opposite) Gym display at a Royal Ballet School matinée in 1961. The group includes David Morse, Kerrison Cooke and David Wall. (Inset) Julia Farron, standing at rear, in rehearsal for 'Nursery Suite' as performed by Vic-Wells Ballet School scholarship pupils at Sadler's Wells Theatre in 1935. (Above, left) Antoinette Sibley as Swanilda and Graham Usher as Franz in 'Coppélia' at the first school matinée in 1959; (right) pupils of the Junior School in 'The Nutcracker' at the Royal Opera House, 1968.

(Right) At daily class on tour, with Anita Landa, Ballet Mistress of Sadler's Wells Royal Ballet. (Below) Jill Gregory, Ballet Mistress, Michael Somes, Principal Répétiteur, and Norman Morrice, Director, of the Royal Ballet, with members of the corps de ballet.
(Opposite, above) Ashley Lawrence conducting the orchestra of Sadler's Wells Royal Ballet on tour in Greece, 1977 ; (below) Kenneth MacMillan rehearsing 'Gloria'.

BATON AND BARRE

Behind every Royal Ballet performance lies constant painstaking work from teachers, ballet masters and mistresses, répétiteurs, all closely in collaboration with the artistic directors Norman Morrice and Peter Wright. Daily class with Company teachers keeps technique in trim. Class for the Covent Garden Company is normally held in the professionally planned surroundings of a studio at the Upper School. For Sadler's Wells Royal Ballet, when they are on tour, classes are often held on stage in the theatre where they are appearing, with portable barres but no mirrors. Otherwise they use their fine new studios at Sadler's Wells.

New ballets are rehearsed with the creating choreographers or, if they are acquisitions, with a proxy producer or a choreologist. Choreology is the method of dance notation used throughout The Royal Ballet, conceived and developed by Rudolf and Joan Benesh.

Older works are in the care of répétiteurs such as Michael Somes, who is a specialist in Ashton's ballets but also thoroughly familiar with the rest of the repertoire. Ballet Masters and Mistresses see that performance standards are maintained. Music is an essential part of ballet and the work of Music Director, conductors, orchestra and rehearsal pianists has to be completely coordinated into Company life.

Sets and costumes are also a vital element. The task of translating the artist's designs into practical terms of dresses and back- or front-cloths lies with the scene painters and wardrobe staff. The wardrobe also have the care of costumes already made: altering, mending, cleaning are constant jobs in London and on tour. Additionally, there are many specialist craft areas: wig-making, jewellery, armoury, shoe-making, dyeing of fabrics, prop making.

In the overall picture of the Company, the people on stage or back stage are not the only ones involved. Administration, front of house staff, box office staff, press office and marketing office all play their part. The public learns about the Company by a combination of efforts, through publicity via the press, through posters, mailing lists and advertising and of course by reading the assessments of ballet critics in national or regional newspapers or journals. Each performance is the result of the united work of a wide variety of people pursuing related careers, even though it is the dancers who capture our imagination.

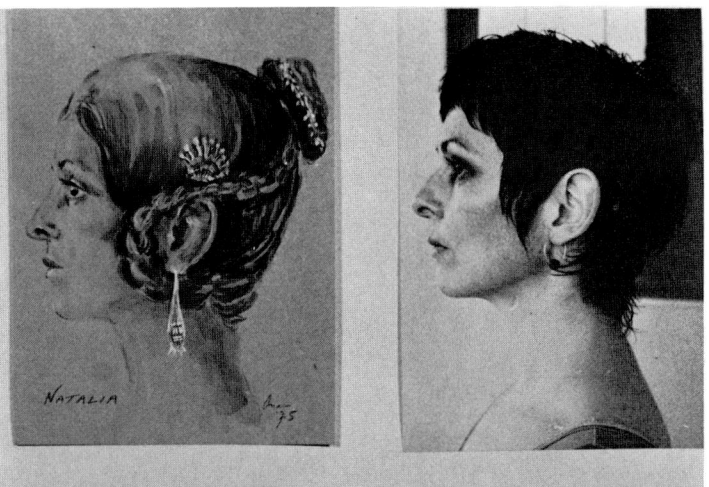

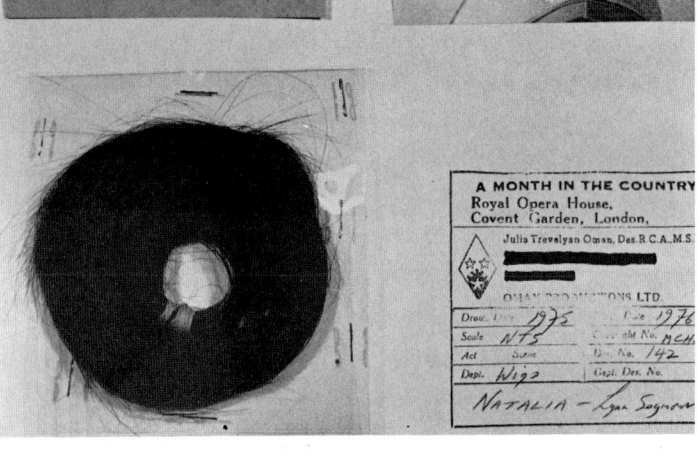

(Opposite) Sir John Tooley, General Director of the Royal Opera House, at centre, with Norman Morrice, left, and Peter Wright, at the 50th Anniversary press conference, 1981; Cover of 'About the House', the magazine of the Friends of Covent Garden. (Left) Wig chart for Lynn Seymour as Natalia in 'A Month in the Country'.
(Below, left) Nesta Brown, in charge of footwear for The Royal Ballet; (right) Lili Sobieralska, Wardrobe Mistress of Sadler's Wells Royal Ballet.

IMAGE

(Below) Televising the Vic-Wells Ballet, c1937. (Right) Margaret Dale, with shooting scripts, demonstrating during rehearsals for one of her television productions. (Below, right) 'Ballet Class', televised in 1964. From left, Georgina Parkinson, Derek Rencher, Peter Wright (Ballet Master), Lynn Seymour, Doreen Wells, Christopher Gable. (Opposite, above) Filming 'Ondine' at the Royal Opera House, 1959; (below) Michael Coleman as Jeremy Fisher in 'Tales of Beatrix Potter', 1971.

A wider audience has enjoyed The Royal Ballet on film and television than in the theatre, both media having been exploited considerably over the years. The first television programme by the Vic-Wells Ballet was on 11 November 1936, in excerpts from *Job*, and programmes were fairly regularly transmitted from Alexandra Palace up to World War II. The first postwar programme by BBC Television was of Sadler's Wells Theatre Ballet in *Assembly Ball* in June 1946.

Many producers have been involved but from 1958 Margaret Dale was responsible for a succession of important telefilms of the Company's repertoire. There have also been excellent documentaries. The outstanding *Ballet Class* (March 1964), produced by Margaret Dale with Peter Wright as Ballet Master, had a line-up of dancers that included Park, Seymour, Wells, Dowell and Gable, and said all that needs to be said about routine technical work.

Dancers of the Vic-Wells Ballet, among them Fonteyn, appeared in the film *Escape Me Never* (1935). One or two documentary films were made in the forties including *Steps of the Ballet* (1948) by the Crown Film Unit.

Feature-length films of ballets were to come. Dr Paul Czinner directed *The Royal Ballet* (released 1960) comprising *Ondine*, *The Firebird* and *Le Lac des Cygnes Act II*, with Fonteyn and Somes. *An Evening with the Royal Ballet*, directed by Anthony Asquith and Anthony Havelock-Allan, followed in 1964 and contained *Les Sylphides*, *Aurora's Wedding*, *La Valse* and *Le Corsaire* pas de deux with Fonteyn and Nureyev. Czinner directed *Romeo and Juliet*, again with Fonteyn and Nureyev, in 1966.

Along with the more orthodox films a unique and delightful venture, *Tales of Beatrix Potter* (1971) featured artistic creation rather than ciné-reportage. Ashton's extraordinarily clever dances for the Potter characters, tailored to suit story, music and costume, are well exemplified in Coleman's perfect Jeremy Fisher solo.

INFLUENCE

(Top) **Peggy van Praagh, Artistic Director, Ray Powell, Ballet Master, with Geoffrey Ingram, Company Administrator of The Australian Ballet, in 1964. (Above) Pupils of the Turkish National Academy of Ballet, founded by Ninette de Valois in 1947.**

The metaphor of the stone in the pool with its widely spreading rings certainly holds good for The Royal Ballet. Its influence, through directors, ballet masters, teachers and dancers has been more far-reaching than that of any ballet organisation of our time.

Former Royal Ballet dancers have created or directed The Australian Ballet (Van Praagh, Helpmann and the present associate directors Bryan Ashbridge and Ray Powell) and the National Ballet of Canada (Franca and currently Alexander Grant). The National Ballet of Turkey grew from the school founded in Istanbul by de Valois. The New Zealand Ballet was formed by Rowena Jackson and Philip Chatfield. David Poole is Artistic Director of CAPAB, Cape Town.

The Stuttgart Ballet was made famous by John Cranko, and its present Director, Marcia Haydée, was at the Royal Ballet School, as was Richard Cragun. MacMillan's term in West Berlin was illustrious. Alan Carter spent five years in Munich and worked with other overseas companies.

John Field had a lively four-year period at La Scala Milan and Brenda Last recently spent some time as Director of the Norwegian Ballet. Individual dancers have represented the Royal Ballet style abroad in guest artist appearances, in seasonal engagements, and in concert groups. Many now teach, in America and elsewhere.

Works from the repertoire have been staged by many companies. The Joffrey Ballet, for one, has been a keen collector, especially of Ashton ballets.

The roll-call of names over the Company's fifty years is a long one. It is to The Royal Ballet's credit that so many of its artists have made solid contributions to various aspects of world dance.

(Above) The Stuttgart Ballet: Marcia Haydée as Katherina, Richard Cragun as Petruchio, in 'The Taming of the Shrew'. (Below) Alexander Grant, Artistic Director of the National Ballet of Canada, with Frederick Ashton rehearsing 'The Two Pigeons'.

REPERTORY

An asterisk (*) denotes ballets created for the Company; m = matinée; e = evening; Ch = Choreography; NP = New Productions; TC = Touring Company; P = Première; pdd = pas de deux; pdt = pas de trois.

This covers productions of both Companies since 1928. *The Royal Ballet* (Covent Garden) evolved as follows: 13 Dec 1928 Old Vic Opera Ballet; 29 Dec '30 Vic-Sadler's Wells Opera Ballet; 5 May '31 Vic-Wells Ballet; May 1940 (on tour of Holland) Sadler's Wells Ballet; 16 Jan '57 The Royal Ballet. *Sadler's Wells Royal Ballet* (Islington) evolved as follows: 8 April 1946 (first full evening of ballet) Sadler's Wells Opera Ballet; 20 Sept '47 Sadler's Wells Theatre Ballet; 16 Jan '57 The Royal Ballet (formerly Sadler's Wells Theatre Ballet)'; Sep 1970 The Royal Ballet New Group; 28 Sep '76 Sadler's Wells Royal Ballet.

THE ROYAL BALLET

1928
Dec 13 — Petits Riens, Les*
1929
May 9 — Picnic, The (revised 1930 as Faun, The)*
Dec 19 — Hommage aux Belles Viennoises*
1930
Dec 18 — Suite of Dances*
1931
May 5 — Danse Sacrée et Danse Profane
Jackdaw and the Pigeons, The*
Faust, Scène de ballet*
21 — Cephalus and Procris
Sept 22 — Regatta*
Job
Nov 23 — Fête Polonaise
Dec 16 — Jew in the Bush, The*
1932
Jan 30m — Narcissus and Echo*
Kout
Mar 4 — Spectre de la Rose, Le
Italian Suite*
8 — Sylphides, Les
11 — Enchanted Grove, The*
19e — Nursery Suite*
Oct 5 — Lac des Cygnes, Le, Act II
11 — Douanes*
17 — Lord of Burleigh, The
Nov 1 — Origin of Design, The
15 — Scorpions of Ysit, The
1933
Jan 17 — Pomona
Feb 7 — Birthday of Oberon, The*
Mar 21 — Coppélia (Acts I/II)
Sept 26 — Wise and Foolish Virgins, The*
Blue Bird, The, pdd (Enchanted Princess, The)
Oct 24 — Sleeping Princess, The, pdd (Aurora pdd)
Carnaval
30 — Création du Monde, La (Ch de Valois)
Dec 5 — Rendezvous, Les*
Lac des Cygnes, Le, pdt
1934
Jan 1 — Giselle
30 — Casse-Noisette
Apr 3 — Haunted Ballroom, The*
Oct 9 — Jar, The*
Nov 20 — Lac des Cygnes, Le
Dec 19 — Uncle Remus*
1935
Mar 26 — Rio Grande
May 20 — Rake's Progress, The*
Oct 8 — Façade
Nov 26 — Baiser de la Fée, Le (Ch Ashton)*

1936
Jan 10 — Gods Go a' Begging, The*
Feb 11 — Apparitions*
Apr 17 — Barabau*
Oct 13 — Prometheus*
Nov 10 — Nocturne*
1937
Feb 16 — Patineurs, Les*
Apr 27 — Wedding Bouquet, A*
June 15 — Checkmate*
1938
Jan 27 — Horoscope*
Apr 7 — Roi Nu, Le*
May 10 — Judgement of Paris, The*
Nov 10 — Harlequin in the Street
1939
Feb 2 — Sleeping Princess, The
Apr 27 — Cupid and Psyche*
1940
Jan 23 — Dante Sonata*
Apr 15 — Coppélia (NP Acts I/II/III)
24 — Wise Virgins, The*
July 4 — Prospect Before Us, The*
1941
Jan 27 — Wanderer, The*
May 28 — Orpheus and Eurydice*
1942
Jan 14 — Comus*
May 19 — Hamlet*
Nov 24 — Birds, The*
1943
Apr 6 — Quest, The*
Oct 25 — Promenade*
1944
June 20 — Festin de l'Araignée, Le*
Oct 26 — Miracle in the Gorbals*
1946
Feb 20 — Sleeping Beauty, The (NP)
Apr 10 — Adam Zero*
24 — Symphonic Variations*
June 12 — Giselle (NP)
Nov 12 — Sirènes, Les*
1947
Feb 6 — Three-Cornered Hat, The
27 — Boutique Fantasque, La
Nov 26 — Mam'zelle Angot
1948
Feb 11 — Scènes de Ballet*
May 20 — Don Quixote, pdd
June 25 — Clock Symphony*
Nov 25 — Don Juan*
Dec 23 — Cinderella*
1950
Feb 20 — Don Quixote (Ch de Valois)*
Apr 5 — Ballet Imperial (from 1973, Piano Concerto No 2)
May 5 — Ballabile*
1951
Apr 5 — Daphnis and Chloë*
July 9 — Tiresias*
Dec 12 — Donald of the Burthens*
1952
Mar 4 — Mirror for Witches, A*
Apr 4 — Bonne-Bouche*
Sept 3 — Sylvia*
Dec 18 — Lac des Cygnes, Le (NP)
1953
Mar 3 — Shadow, The*
Apr 9 — Veneziana*
June 2 — Homage to the Queen*
1954
Mar 2 — Coppélia (NP)
Aug 23 — Firebird, The

1955
Jan 6 — Rinaldo and Armida*
Variations on a Theme of Purcell*
Apr 1 — Madame Chrysanthème*
June 9 — Lady and the Fool, The
1956
Feb 15 — Péri, La*
Mar 1 — Noctambules*
May 5 — Birthday Offering*
Aug 27 — Miraculous Mandarin, The*
1957
Jan 1 — Prince of the Pagodas, The*
Mar 26 — Petrushka
Sept 17 — Solitaire
1958
Aug 20 — Agon (Ch MacMillan)*
Oct 27 — Ondine*
Dec 11 — Fête Etrange, La
1959
Mar 5 — Harlequin in April
10 — Valse, La
13 — Danses Concertantes
Sept 2 — Belle Dame sans Merci, La
22 — Pineapple Poll
Oct 19 — Antigone*
1960
Jan 28 — Fille Mal Gardée, La*
Mar 1 — Raymonda 'Scène d'Amour'
Apr 12 — Baiser de la Fée, Le (Ch MacMillan)
Sept 30 — Giselle (NP)
1961
Sept 15 — Diversions*
Jabez and the Devil*
Dec 12 — Perséphone*
1962
May 3 — Napoli Divertissement
Flower Festival at Genzano, pdd
Rite of Spring, The*
July 11 — Good-Humoured Ladies, The
Oct 16 — Two Pigeons, The
Nov 3e — Corsaire, Le, pdd
Dec 13 — Invitation, The
1963
Feb 15 — Symphony*
Mar 12 — Night Tryst*
Marguerite and Armand*
26 — Elektra*
Nov 27 — Bayadère, La
Dec 12 — Swan Lake (NP)
1964
Apr 2 — Dream, The*
Images of Love*
May 7 — Serenade
Dec 2 — Biches, Les
1965
Feb 9 — Romeo and Juliet*
Mar 24 — Monotones pdt*
(from 1966, Monotones No 2)
Laurentia, pas de six
Polovtsian Dances from Prince Igor
1966
Feb 10 — Brandenburg Nos 2 and 4*
18 — Card Game
Mar 23 — Noces, Les
Apr 25 — Monotones No 1*
May 19 — Song of the Earth
Nov 15 — Apollo
1967
Jan 25 — Shadowplay*
Feb 23 — Paradise Lost*
Dec 18 — Sylvia (one-act version)

"I tell yer, it ain't safe to be abaht the Garden now the blinkin' ballet's back!"

Cartoon by Lee, from The Evening News the day after the reopening of the Royal Opera House, Covent Garden, on 20 February 1946.

REPERTORY

**Frederick Ashton rehearsing Merle
Park in the tango from 'Façade'.**

1955
Jan 18 Danses Concertantes★
Apr 23m Patineurs, Les
May 26 House of Birds★
Oct 13 Saudades★
1956
Jan 16 Coppélia (NP)
May 9 Somnambulism
June 7 Solitaire★
July 28 Giselle Act II
Aug 18 Giselle
1957
Jan 28 Apparitions
Dec 26 Blue Rose, A★
Angels, The★
28m Veneziana
1958
Jan 2 Burrow, The★
June 27 Lac des Cygnes, Le
Sept 23 Don Quixote, pdd
Nov 4 Hamlet
1959
Sept 14 Sleeping Beauty, The
16 Belle Dame sans Merci, La
Dec 10m Sweeney Todd★
1960
Nov 10 Invitation, The★
1961
Feb 14 Deux Pigeons, Les★
(Two Pigeons, The)
Apr 18 Checkmate
1962
Oct 27m Flower Festival at Genzano
pas de deux
Napoli, Divertissement
Nov 9 Fille Mal Gardée, La
Dec 14 Toccata★
1963
May 17 Bal des Voleurs, Le
1964
Feb 12 Création du Monde, La (Ch
MacMillan)
July 10 Raymonda
Oct 29 Summer's Night★
Quintet
1965
Feb 5 Tribute, The★
May 18 Swan Lake (NP)
1966
May 7 Raymonda Act III
Dec 2 Dream, The
1967
Feb 10 Sinfonietta★
May 26 Concerto
1968
Jan 31 Boutique Fantasque, La
Mam'zelle Angot
May 15 Giselle (NP)
28 Monotones Nos 1 and 2
Nov 25 Knight Errant★
1969
Jan 17 Intrusion
In the Beginning★

Dec 5 Lazarus
1970
Jan 30 From Waking Sleep★
May 13 Symphonie Pastorale, La★
June 6 Creatures of Prometheus, The★
Nov 9 Apollo
Field Figures★
Symphonic Variations
12 Lilac Garden
27 Checkpoint★
1971
Feb 8 Overture★
10 Diversions
Grand Tour, The★
June 2 Hermanas, Las
7 St Thomas' Wake
9 Ante Room★
Oct 12 Caprichos
19 Maids, The
1972
Feb 15 Mirror Walkers, The, pdd
22 O.W.★
Apr 1m Side Show
26 Laurentia pas de six
29m Grosse Fuge
May 19 Ballade★
26 Triad
June 15 Romeo and Juliet,
Balcony, pdd
July 28 Siesta★
30 Valse Eccentrique
Oct 12 Poltroon, The★
26 In a Summer Garden★
Nov 23 Tragédie à Verone,
Balcony, pdd
1973
Feb 27 Allegro Brillante
Mar 2 Twilight
Sacred Circles★
5 Raymonda, Scene d'Amour
16 Migration★
May 2 Tilt
Aug 8 Prodigal Son
Oct 3 Card Game
23 Sword of Alsace★
1974
Feb 12 Septet Extra
Mar 8 Charlotte Brontë★
May 2 Entertainers, The★
14 Wedding Bouquet, A
Oct 2 Unfamiliar Playground★
1975
Feb 14 Arpège
Shukumei★
Apr 15 Coppélia (NP)
Sept 5 Amor Brujo, El★
1976
Jan 30 Pandora★
June 2 Lulu★
30 Sleeping Beauty, The, Act III
(Aurora's Wedding)
Oct 4 Four Temperaments, The
12 Summertide★

19 Rashomon★
1977
Feb 11 Birdscape★
Apr 21 Court of Love, The★
May 5 Gemini
Aug 26 Concerto Barocco
Sept 20 Soft Blue Shadows
1978
Feb 10 Elite Syncopations
Mar 16 Outsider, The★
May 3 Brouillards
12 Game Piano★
Sept 26 Take Five★
6.6.78★
Oct 10 Intimate Letters★
1979
Feb 9 Coppélia (NP)
Mar 16 Meadow of Proverbs★
30m Rhyme nor Reason
Aug 20 Punch and the Street Party★
24 Playground★
1980
Feb 7 Papillon
15 Homage to Chopin★
Pavane
Mar 28 Day into Night★
Apr 17 Paquita
June 20 Catch
Dec 9 Polonia
16 The Taming of the Shrew

The Company also appeared in the following Covent Garden productions during their seasons at the Royal Opera House.

1960
Dec 14 Cinderella
1963
May 6 Sylvia
1970
Apr 23 Job

PICTURE CREDITS

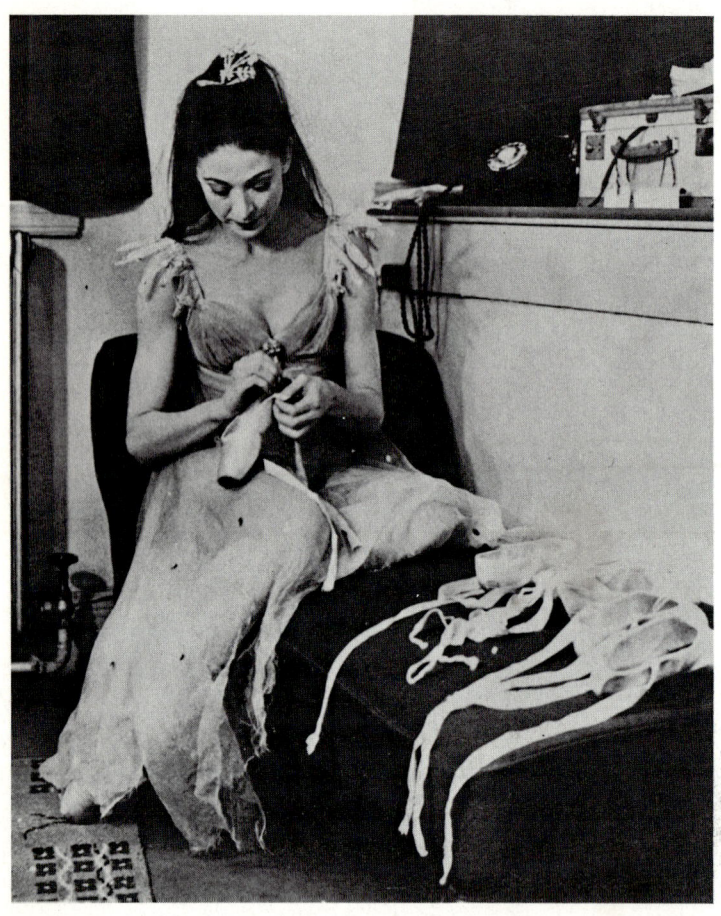

Margot Fonteyn in her dressing room preparing for a performance of 'Ondine', 1959.

Front Cover: Antoinette Sibley and Anthony Dowell in *The Dream*. Houston Rogers/Theatre Museum. Back Cover: *Romeo and Juliet* Act I, the Ballroom Scene. Zoë Dominic. Title Page (left & right): Ninette de Valois at Class, 1940. Gordon Anthony/Theatre Museum. Half Title: Members of the Sadler's Wells Theatre Ballet by the river at Cambridge, late 1940s. Edward Mandinian/Theatre Museum. Imprint Page: Cartoon from *The Ottawa Citizen,* 1949. Page 7: Montage Leslie Spatt.

The following pictures, listed in page number order, are from the Theatre Museum: page 9 *Narcisse* (Sasha); 12 Baylis (J. W. Debenham); 13, 14 Sadler's Wells; 15 programmes, *Danse Sacrée* (Debenham); 16 *Job* (Morter), *Sylphides*; 17 *Coppélia* and *Douanes* (Debenham); 18 *Giselle* and Lanchester (Debenham); 19 *Casse-Noisette*; 20 *Haunted Ballroom* (Debenham); 20/21 *Lac* (Debenham); 22 Fonteyn and *Rio Grande* (Debenham); 23 leaflet, *Rake* (Debenham); 24 *Façade* (Debenham), Farron (Gordon Anthony); 25 Ashton (G. Anthony), *Baiser* (Debenham); 28 *Gods Go a' Begging* and Company at Sadler's Wells (Debenham); 29 *Nocturne* (Debenham); 30 *Patineurs* (Merlyn Severn), *Wedding Bouquet* (G. Anthony); 31 *Checkmate* (M. Severn); 32 Fonteyn in *Giselle, Lac, Rendezvous* (G. Anthony); 33 *Horoscope* (Debenham); 34 Apotheosis and Blue Birds (G. Anthony); 35 Fairies (G. Anthony), programme; 36 *Dante Sonata*, Sophie Fedorovitch (G. Anthony); 37 *Coppélia*, Chappell (G. Anthony); 38 *Prospect* (G. Anthony); 40 *The Wanderer* (Ernest); 41 *Orpheus* (G. Anthony); 42 *Comus* (Germaine Kanova); 46 Helpmann, *Promenade* (G. Anthony); 47 *Miracle* (Mandinian); 48/49 *Sleeping Beauty* (Mandinian); 51 *Assembly Ball, Mardi Gras* (Mandinian); 52 Massine (Mandinian); 53 *Boutique Fantasque* (Mandinian); 54 *Fête Etrange* (de Marney); 55 Selina; 56 Helpmann (Mandinian); 60 *Daphnis* (Houston Rogers); 62 *Coppélia, Pineapple Poll*, Mosaval (de Marney); 64 *Homage to the Queen* (H. Rogers); 65 *Firebird, Coppélia* (H. Rogers); 66 *Lady and Fool* (de Marney); 68 *Danses Concertantes* (de Marney), *Giselle* (H. Rogers); 69 van Praagh (de Marney); 72 *Petrushka* (H. Rogers); 74 *Ondine* (H. Rogers); 75 *Sleeping Beauty* (H. Rogers); 76 *Fille*, Nerina, Holden (H. Rogers); 77 Opera Ballet (H. Rogers); 78 *The Invitation* (H. Rogers); 79 *Two Pigeons* (H. Rogers); 82 *Fille* (H. Rogers); 83 *Swan Lake* (H. Rogers); 85 *Marguerite and Armand* (H. Rogers); 88 *Serenade, Les Biches* (H. Rogers); 90/91 *Romeo and Juliet* (H. Rogers); 92/93 *Cinderella* (H. Rogers); 96 *Les Noces* (H. Rogers); 98 *Shadowplay* (H. Rogers); 100/101 *Giselle* (H. Rogers); 102/103 *Sleeping Beauty* Lilac Fairy and Waltz (H. Rogers); 104/105 *Enigma Variations*, Company, and Bergsma (H. Rogers); 131 Matinée and Junior School (H. Rogers); 137 *Ondine* (H. Rogers); 144 Fonteyn (H. Rogers).

The following photographers and agencies are listed in alphabetical order. BBC: 96 *Monotones*; 136 TV, 1937, and Ballet Class. Roland Bond: 98 *Concerto*; 106 Wall/Thorogood and *Pasiphaë*. Graham Brandon: 128 *Gloria*. Joe Bulatis: De Valois; John Cowan: 74 Cranko, Sibley. Anthony Crickmay: 99 *Coppélia*; 113 Jenner; 114 *Grosse Fuge*; 114 *Twilight*; 122/123 *Mayerling*, Collier; Larsen. Alan Cunliffe: 124 *The Outsider*. The Daily Telegraph: 44 Princesses. Dance & Dancers: 138 Australian Ballet. The Dancing Times: 8 Ad; 10 *Tragedy of Fashion* (Bertram Park); 12 Ad; 15 Workers' Class; 16 *Regatta* (Navana); 66 *Blood Wedding* (Paul Wilson); 72 Grigoriev. Fredrika Davis: 88 *The Dream*. Zoë Dominic: 71 *Prince of the Pagodas*; 80 Class at Bolshoi, *Ondine* at Kirov; 86 Corps de ballet; 95 *Raymonda*; 109 *Field Figures*; 111 *Rake, Grand Tour*; 114 *The Maids*; 130 Gym display. EMI: 137 Beatrix Potter. Evening Standard: 132 Gregory with corps; 140 Cartoon. Felix Fonteyn: 65 *Sylvia*. Harvard Theatre Collection: 54 *Valses Nobles* (Angus McBean); 68/69 *Solitaire* (Angus McBean). Mike Humphrey: 105 *Enigma*, Dowell. Colin Jones: 83 Touring. London News Agency: 38/39 Tour, 1940. Ross MacGibbon: 117 New York. Mansell Collection: 21 *Carnaval* (E. O. Hoppé); 130 Vic-Wells School. Pictorial Press: 34 Sergeyev. Radio Times Hulton: 50 *Symphonic Variations* (Baron); 52 *Mam'zelle Angot* (Baron); 70 Brian Shaw (Baron). Stuart Robinson: 110 *Anastasia*, Seymour. Roy Round: 73 *The Burrow*; 84 *Rite of Spring*. Royal Ballet School: 13 *Les Petits Riens*; 41 *Orpheus*. Royal Opera House: 18 *Les Rendezvous*. Scott & Wilkinson: 12 *Rout*. John Sculpher: 132 On tour; 135 Wardrobe Mistress. David Sim: 74 *Rake*. Donald Southern: 89 *Défilé*; 134 Press Conference; 135 Wig chart, Ballet shoes. Leslie Spatt: 85 Nureyev; 97 *Song of the Earth*; 98/99 *Nutcracker*; 103 Dowell Sibley; 105 *Enigma* Sibley; 106 Nureyev; 108 *Dances at a Gathering*; 109 *Apollo*; 110 *Anastasia* Seymour; 112 *Afternoon of a Faun, Triad*; 113 Makarova; 114 *Card Game*; 116 *Manon*; 117 *Elite*; 118 *The Concert*; 119 *Month in the Country, Voluntaries*; 120 *Rashomon*; 121 *Summertide*; 122/123 *Mayerling*, Wall/Seymour, Jefferies/Thorogood, Ellis; 125 Fonteyn, Helpmann; 126 *Papillon*; 127 *Day into Night, Paquita*; 129 *Sleeping Beauty*; 133 MacMillan; 143 Park, Ashton *Façade*. The Tatler: 39 Fontaine; 46 cartoon. Thames TV: 101 *Giselle*. The Times: 11 Review; 14 *Carmen*; 93 (inset); 138 Turkish Academy. Tunbridge-Sedgwick: 42 *The Birds*; 42/43 *Hamlet*; 44 *The Quest*; 45 Fonteyn, Grey, *Lac*. Moira Walters: 129 *Rhapsody*; Hans Wild: 57 *Scenes de Ballet*; Alex Wilson: 124 *Playground*. G.B.L. Wilson: 136 Margaret Dale. Reg Wilson: 87, 94 *Swan Lake*. Roger Wood: 57 *Cinderella*; 60 *Ballet Imperial*; 70 *Birthday Offering*.

Note: The Repertory Statistics on pages 140-42 were originally compiled for *The Royal Ballet: The first 50 years*, published by Threshold Books/Sotheby Parke Bernet, 1981.